MAGICAL PATHWORKING

TECHNIQUES OF ACTIVE IMAGINATION

About the Author

Nick Farrell was initiated into the Builders of the Adytum and the Order of the Table Round (a Golden Dawn side order). He now runs a temple in the tradition of the Esoteric Order of the Golden Dawn, and conducts lectures and workshops throughout the world.

To Write to the Author

If you wish to contact the author or would like more information about this book, please write to the author in care of Llewellyn Worldwide and we will forward your request. Both the author and publisher appreciate hearing from you and learning of your enjoyment of this book and how it has helped you. Llewellyn Worldwide cannot guarantee that every letter written to the author can be answered, but all will be forwarded. Please write to:

Nick Farrell
⅍ Llewellyn Worldwide
P.O. Box 64383, Dept. 0-7383-0407-5
St. Paul, MN 55164-0383, U.S.A.

Please enclose a self-addressed stamped envelope for reply,
or $1.00 to cover costs. If outside U.S.A., enclose an
international postal reply coupon.

Many of Llewellyn's authors have websites
with additional information and resources.
For more information, please visit our website at
http://www.llewellyn.com

MAGICAL PATHWORKING
TECHNIQUES OF ACTIVE IMAGINATION

NICK FARRELL

2004
Llewellyn Publications
St. Paul, Minnesota 55164–0383, U.S.A.

First Edition
First Printing, 2004

Cover art © Photodisc & Digital Stock
Cover design by Gavin Dayton Duffy
Interior illustrations by Llewellyn Art Department
Editing by T. Bilstad

Library of Congress Cataloging-in-Publication Data
Farrell, Nick, 1965–
    Magical pathworking : techniques of active imagination / Nick Farrell.—1st ed.
      p.   cm.
    Includes bibliographical references.
    ISBN 0-7387-0407-5
      1. Magic. 2. Imagination. I. Title.

  BF1621.F37 2004
  133.4'3—dc22   2004048461

Llewellyn Publications
A Division of Llewellyn Worldwide, Ltd.
P.O. Box 64383, Dept.0-7387-0407-5
St. Paul, MN 55164-0383, U.S.A.
www.llewellyn.com

Printed in the United States of America

Other Books by this Author

Making Talismans
Llewellyn Publications, 2001

To Marian Green, writer and occultist,
who has selflessly worked to foster the
Western Mystery Tradition in the United Kingdom.

Contents

Chapter Eight . . . 205

Life is but a Dream

List of Figures

Acknowledgments

This book is the result of countless experiments with pathworking and the avenues of the mind. The book's success is due to the patience of many whom worked with the techniques, even though we were initially uncertain of its effects. To these brave people I acknowledge their contribution, particularly Jane and Anna. Peter Gabriel's album *Us*, particularly the song "Digging in the Dirt," was an inspirational soundtrack to the process we were developing.

Rufus Harrington enabled me to see that some of the life-healing techniques in this book could be used in modern conventional therapy and counseling.

Marian Green was the first to get me interested in the workings of the magical imagination and the writers W. E. Butler, Dion Fortune, and David Goddard were all influences.

On the Golden Dawn side I am indebted to the work of Chic and Tabatha Cicero, who have managed to keep the tradition alive into the twenty-first century. Thanks also to Kate Fairhurst for her ruthless proofing of the first draft.

Without all these people it is unlikely that this book could ever have been written, or completed. Indeed my life would not have been as interesting as it has been without them.

Introduction

Imagination has always been important to me. As a child, I often created worlds and disappeared into them when the pressures of life were too much. Being asthmatic with a complete disinterest in sports, growing up in New Zealand made such imaginary worlds an increasingly attractive escape from the bullies and "weird waltzes" of early relationships.

Like many of those whom the writer Colin Wilson would label "outsiders," I was a people watcher, and inhaled psychology books to learn more about the way they worked.

In my late teens my knowledge grew, and upon entering into my adult life these daydreams became less important, and my psychological knowledge just became another tool for understanding the life around me. But occult study reactivated my interest in these subjects. Books by Marian Green, Dolores Ashcroft-Nowicki, and John and Caitlin Mathews started to convince me that these imaginary worlds of mine were not only real, but also had a direct magical purpose. The

Builders of the Adytum, my first magical school, taught me that these visualizations could actually change my material world.

In those days "pathworking" was still discussed in the hushed whispers that followed the public disclosure of a technique once closely guarded by the mystery schools. Now, only fifteen years later, pathworking is so commonplace that it is almost regarded as a beginner's technique.

Few have tried to work out what is happening with these magical imagination states or even teach how to create them. This book aims to present what I have learned about pathworking and show how they can be constructed for the maximum effectiveness.

Pathworkings are only the start of magical imagination techniques; indeed, its uses are an untapped well waiting to be explored by magicians in the twenty-first century. This book will show that there is a direct link between psychological states and those environments created in the imagination. Neurotic complexes that do so much to spoil and limit our lives have the same reality in our imaginations and, therefore, it should be possible to correct these faults using magical imagination techniques. Instead of waiting for a person to dream to hear the voice of his or her unconscious, creative imagination would enable a person to have direct access to the unconscious mind—not only two-way communication, but also a way of repairing mental faults.

The only way to prove this theory was with experimentation. Over a number of years a group of magicians and friends of mine worked through various techniques, finding that pathworking was indeed a door to our psychological states. Healing these neurotic complexes initially seemed so easy that we overcompensated in the amount of work we tried to correct. We forgot to take into account the tremendous fallout that followed each experiment. Repairing a complex in a day that has taken years to build had a delayed result that was felt months or years later, and at the time we were doing one of these workings a week (not something I recommend now!).

After the dust settled, we were completely different people, free from many of the shackles that had bound us. It was during this period that I was a member of the Servants of the Light (SOL), which ran a correspondence course using the concept of using a pathworking to create a mental environment that represents your inner self. This "Inner Kingdom" was set in a King Arthur mythos, with a castle representing the physical body of a person. Written by W. E. Butler, and embellished by Dolores Ashcroft-Nowicki, the correspondence course aimed to awaken magical energies within a person to enable spiritual development. (The guts of the SOL course was published by David Goddard in his book *Tower of Alchemy*.) But what interested me was that it created an Inner Kingdom, which had to be maintained for some time (the course lasted five years). During this course, my Inner Kingdom not only taught me spiritual things, but also gave me a symbolic insight into the way my outer life was going.

If an Inner Kingdom were built, it would be possible to see the world as my unconscious saw it. What was learned from that unique perspective was that I was the ruler of my own Inner Kingdom, and if I made a change at the unconscious level, it was possible to change my life.

My experimentation with magical imagination has continued. I have subsequently handed the technique over several counselors and they have also found it effective. More recently, I have chosen to adopt the system of the Esoteric Order of the Golden Dawn, a magical order that formed at the turn of the nineteenth century. And in these teachings I found an explanation to many of the magical imagination techniques I used before. (It was these Golden Dawn techniques that inspired the poet W. B. Yeats.)

The mystical use of pathworkings as a method of contacting the divine within has become more important. This use of pathworking is still rarely talked about, as the techniques for its use are considered too dangerous for beginners. I remain skeptical about these fears, as a person experimenting with mystical states will see the divine to his or her own level of understanding. The only danger of pathworking would be to those suffering from mental illness—a state that would be true of anyone pursuing an esoteric path.

There are occultists who might object to the publication of these techniques or the revealing of the secrets of magical imagination, however, it is important that the techniques for magical imagination pathworking be available for those people who really want to work with them. I am a firm believer that "the casting of pearls before swine" is preferable to burying said pearls in a locked box where they cannot be found by anyone. Pearls can be found by those who look for them if these treasures are left out in the open, and will be ignored by those who cannot recognize them.

This book also includes actual pathworkings and examples of their utilization. Although these pathworkings have been all tested and work in their own right, the aim of this book is to encourage development and experimentation in this new and exciting esoteric field.

Nick Farrell
Nottingham
December 2001

CHAPTER ONE

Magical Imagination

The term *magical imagination* refers to the art of changing your consciousness to rebuild aspects of your life and self to bring about a transformation of your environment. Everyone builds around them an impression of reality—a unique image of the universe from their own perspective. This universe is built from countless experiences since birth. These are the lessons that we have taught ourselves or accepted as gospel from our parents, teachers, friends, and society. Over the years our universe becomes more defined, meaning that we can handle more of what our life throws at us.

Sometimes that world picture is incorrect. What our parents or teachers present to us as fact is sometimes bigoted or just wrong. Being children, and not having any evidence to challenge that information, we accept "the facts" and paint it into our worldview. Sometimes we build features in our Inner Kingdoms to protect us from hurt. This is particularly true of victims of abuse, who have elaborate defense mechanisms designed to overcome the intense psychological stress such abuse triggers. The behavior patterns learned to avoid the pain of such instances are often applied the rules to our whole Inner Kingdom. Everything that looks similar to the original situation is incorrectly treated in the same way. A lover, with whom you are extremely close, can suddenly become the manipulative father who terrorized your childhood. All it takes is the wrong gesture because, in the rules of this Inner Kingdom, the people who make that hurtful gesture are the bad guys.

Occultism teaches that our mental picture of the universe is such a powerful force for stability that it eventually creates the circumstances that maintain it. In other words, how we see our universe becomes a self-fulfilling prophecy. The person who is rich in spiritual beliefs is likely to be blessed with many experiences with the divine, while those lacking in spiritual beliefs will often not recognize any contact to the divine. But occultism also teaches that since such a universe is built by the imagination (that great magical wand of the magician), so the universe can be changed. Over the millennia, countless different techniques were developed to enable people to master their personal universe using their imagination. These techniques enabled them to change the wiring of their minds to let in things like success, happiness, and well-being.

Imagination has had such a bad press ever since the scientists of the nineteenth century looked for purely materialistic theories to explain the world around them. To these "rational" scientists, imagination equated daydreaming and was therefore unnecessary. Just like a grumpy schoolteacher who tells off a schoolboy for staring out the window, "science" shouted at us to "Pay attention!" without actually realizing what powers imagination had. Science was brilliant at saying what was happening now, but what of the future? Inventions and human developments are 99 percent the work of dreamers and imaginative people.

There is a stigma attached to imagination techniques. I recall a scathing book review of David Goddard's *Tower of Alchemy*, which deals with a good imagination technique. The reviewer said that since

Goddard seemed to believe that if you daydreamed your problems away, all would then be right. The reviewer wondered if this line of reasoning was terribly wrong. *Magical Pathworking* will prove that imagination does and can work wonders.

To show that imagination can work wonders, let us perform an experiment. Shut your eyes and imagine a castle. After a few seconds, open your eyes and describe that castle out loud. You will have a very full picture of what the castle looks like after a few seconds thinking about it. Where did all that information come from? You could argue that it was based on a memory of a castle you might have seen or read in a book. Have you actually visited that castle? If so, have you visited it from that exact vantage point you imagined? I would argue that what you have done is painted the picture using your imagination, and this whole construct was based on a simple phrase "Imagine a castle . . ." All that detail that did not come from your memory came from somewhere else, a part the psychologist Jung would call the unconscious.

It is clear that we are dealing with something more important than just mere fancy. In fact, one of the greatest magicians in the nineteenth century, Dr. William Westcott, who founded the famous magical group the Esoteric Order of the Golden Dawn, said that imagination must be distinguished from fancy, which is "mere roving thoughts, or simply visions." He said that imagination is "an orderly and intentional mental process and result. Imagination is the creative faculty of the human mind, the plastic energy—the Formative Power."[1] Westcott added that the power of imagination to create images enabled it to produce external phenomena by its own energy. "It is an ancient Hermetic dogma that any idea can be made to manifest externally if only by culture, the art of concentration be obtained . . . Man by his creative power through will and thought was more divine than the Angels for he can create and they cannot."

The Mind and the Brain

Like philosophy, those who study the mind fall into two broad camps. There are the rationalists who believe that everything is limited to the world we experience through our senses, and then there are the idealists who argue that the whole of the world is mental.

Many rationalists have tried to say that the brain is the center of consciousness. The most recent notable attempt was in *Astonishing Hypothesis: The Scientific Search for the Soul*,[2] in which the writer Francis Crick argued the mind was the sum total of millions of brain cells.

Most occultists opt for the more philosophically "idealist" idea that all things are thought, and the brain is just an organic radio set that picks up memories and thoughts from outside the body. Medical science may disagree with this particular point, but, equally, it cannot disprove it either. Experiments on patients who were conscious when their brains were operated upon reported having memories, or feeling sensations, when parts of their brains were stimulated. This does not mean that those memories were in the brain, but rather the switches were flicked in the person's brain that connected to the real memory that was outside the physical body. Likewise, when people suffer accidents or mental disabilities that prevent them remembering, or causing them to see things in unusual way, it is because this organic radio has been damaged and cannot see outside itself effectively. Saying that all knowledge is in your brain is like saying all the knowledge of the Internet is in your personal computer. This statement is subjectively correct in that the knowledge ends up on your computer, but if you disconnected your computer from the phone line, you are unlikely to pick up any information.

The ancient Greek philosopher Plato (who inspired many esoteric schools) said in his book *Phaedos* that the mind was imperishable, immortal, and, as such, had knowledge of the universe. In fact, the whole of the universe was the action of a Universal Mind that was creating using imagination. United States comic Bill Hicks summed up how the Universal Mind worked: "We are all one consciousness experiencing itself subjectively. There is no such thing as death, life is only a dream and we are the imagination of ourselves."[3] Your mind is just a reflection or a specialization of that larger Mind. Once you get it out of your head that your mind is your brain, then you can truly start to see how free and immortal you are.

There seem to be clear boundaries between us and a realization of the true nature of this universe. These are walls that define us as separate from the rest of humanity and the universe. Unless we are extremely enlightened or mentally ill, we see ourselves as individuals who have clearly defined boundaries between ourselves and the rest of the world. This is mostly because our consciousness is deliberately limited by the design of creation. We were built to see a very small part of creation and experience it consciously. We are like a meditation on a specific subject being carried out by the Universal Mind.

When we were born, a little part of the immortal Universal Mind was placed at the core of our being. This portion has been called the "ghost in the machine" or the "rider in the chariot," but it is the real you. It experiences matter and the bewildering aspects around it called life, and after a while it forgets its divine self and gets on with existing. You may have noticed something similar when you drive a car. After a while our consciousness expands until we are less the person driving and more an entity called "the car."

Throughout our short history on this planet, humanity has produced people who discover their own divine self and cooperate with the Universal Mind. Firstly, they work out how their own mind works and how they use it. Then they balance themselves away from emotional, intellectual, and social extremes so they may truly express the will of the Universal Mind in their lives. This leads to fulfillment and access to powers that many consider miraculous. This fulfillment enables them to do more within creation. The interesting thing about aligning yourself with the Universal Mind is that it does not make you superspiritual (or even particularly godlike), instead, it makes you more intensely yourself, and you have an interesting life with all the challenges that get thrown at you.

How the Mind Learns

When we are born, the Universal Mind surrounds the physical body on all levels. At the center of this is the spark of divinity from which a personality will develop. This spark forms a link with the developing body, centering itself in one of the energy centers in the heart. Surrounding itself with energy, the spark can pilot the body through life. Initially, it has some difficulty in that this spark of divinity cannot use the developing brain, which has not been programmed yet. What the spark does is quickly train the brain with a set of experiences that enable it to function. Initially a baby's brain will not allow it to have a concept of which it is separate from the surrounding world. The spark has its work cut out in the initial phases as the baby rapidly learns things like up, down, light, and dark. As it does, the baby slowly builds a mental framework for what will become its own Inner Kingdom. It is also during this time that early life patterns are established and crucial programming is performed by the Universal Mind to move the soul toward the life purpose that has mapped out for it. This process takes time and requires the spark to make frequent trips into the Universal Mind to recharge its batteries and process the data it is getting from the brain. This is done during sleep (and possibly explains why babies need so much!).

One of the downsides of this process is that as the Universal Mind depends on the sensory experience of the newly born brain as its anchor on the material plane, it becomes limited and unable to function at its full potential. It forgets and will spend the rest of its physical plane life rediscovering part of what it already knows. This process is accentuated during the next phase when the child accepts that its mother is a separate identity from itself and it has enough of an inner reality to start asserting itself on the physical levels. This usually happens around the age of two (the aptly named "terrible twos"), when the individuality makes its first declarations and yet still lacks the communication skills to articulate its personal needs. This leads to deep frustration for the child. The price for such individuality is a conscious disconnection from the Universal Mind and the reality that the child sees around it. The child still feels the Universal Mind's presence in sleep or daydreaming, but generally the child's focus is on the world around. The child starts to learn by cause and effect, learning, for example, that touching something hot hurts, so touching such an object is a bad idea. It is important to realize that the part of the child that is learning is the brain. The Universal Mind already knows what will happen if it touches a candle flame; it is vital to get the body to realize what will happen. It is not so much learning as remembering what the reality is. It is only by experience that our physical form remembers much of our true reality and our brains gain access to more aspects of the Universal Mind.

Because of the way this process works, humans need experience to develop and grow. Good and bad events flavor our lives, enabling our Inner Kingdoms to grow and become rich. In experiencing more Universal Mind at the heart, the personality grows too.

Associations develop like logic trees, with each experience mapping onto another one. Not only touching a candle flame is bad, touching hot objects becomes bad, and soon other associations become loaded in with the association "bad." An example of this was the famous experiments conducted by Ivan Pavlov, who found that he could condition a dog to slaver on demand by ringing a bell whenever it was presented with food. After a while, the dog was so accustomed to associating the bell with food it would slaver if the bell rang.

Unfortunately, some of these associations are incorrect. For example, a child might see a respected adult recoiling in terror from a spider and assume that spiders were as dangerous as the candle flame.

The association process builds until things that are like the original fear also get the same response. In one politically incorrect experiment conducted in 1920 by Watson and Rayner, the pair took a baby called Albert and showed him a white rat and then made a loud noise. Like Pavlov's dog, poor Albert started to associate the rat with the loud noise, and became frightened every time he saw a white rat. However, Albert's mind also associated the white rat with white fur, rodents, and all small furry things, and so became frightened of these objects too.[4]

But fear is not the only conditioned response. People can be conditioned to do practically anything if they think it is going to avoid them suffering from pain that they have experienced in the past. For example, one woman, verbally abused by her live-in boyfriend for not locking her house's front door, went through an elaborate ritual of making sure the door was locked whenever she left the house. Sometimes it could take some sixty seconds of leaning on the door to make sure it was secured. Later, this pattern extended to checking the handle of the car door, which she performed so rigorously that the handle broke off.

When associative patterns of behavior become so elaborate, they become what psychologist Jung called complexes.[5] People operating in the grips of a complex often find themselves behaving in strange ways, often without knowing why. For example, a boy is struck by his mother for standing on his bed. She fails to give a reason for hitting the boy other than saying a single word, "Dirty." To avoid the pain of being hit again, the boy never stands on the bed but associates the bed with "dirty." The same boy becomes involved in a church group and during a sermon the minister, whom he respects, refers to sex as being "dirty," causing the boy to link the word "sex" with "dirty" and therefore, by association, the word "bed." So it is not surprising that when the boy has his first sexual experience, he has a complex about having sex on a bed. It was only by tracking the association trail backward that one can see was how the boy ended up with this complex.

The mind develops these associations to enable it to provide a rapid reaction to events that unfold in the child's daily life. In fact, your Inner Kingdom is made up of millions of these different complexes, which your mind orders and links together with symbolic language.

Symbols are the Key

The word "symbol" comes from the Late Greek word *symbolon*, meaning "token or sign." A symbol is something that stands for another object, resembling the object in some way. A white dove, for example, is a symbol of peace, because in the biblical story of Noah a dove carried an olive branch to indicate that the tempest was over. However, symbols are much more than that. In a world, which is built by a mind, a symbol is a language that can key you into various thoughts and feelings built up over millennia of human history.

Throughout a study of occultism you will see symbols drawn on paper, on talismans, in magical books. Some of these are common, like a crucifix, while others are more elaborate, such as the pentacles contained in the medieval spell book *The Key of Solomon*. Symbols are designed to stimulate the mind so that it can contact the deeper, more powerful realms of the unconscious Universal Mind.

A symbol links associations together. For example, in your mind all canines will be linked with a symbol of a dog. When you see a dog, your mind will instantly access those files that are associated with it. Upon opening the file, it will see all the associations, good or bad, that you might have about dogs (which are themselves stored under appropriate symbols). Some symbols are unique to you. These are ones that you have built yourself from your own experiences. Someone who was bitten by a dog in his or her childhood might associate the dog symbol as a bringer of pain and fear, while another might have happier connections and see a dog as a symbol of friendship.

There are two types of symbols. Firstly, there are primary, or archetypal, symbols, which are basic and designed to only stress a single idea.

Secondary symbols are simply primary symbols with added details to stress certain meanings that may be obscured in the drawing of the archetypal symbol. Take, for example, a drawing of an equal-armed cross. This primary symbol says (basically) there are four elements that, when they meet in balance, enable a fifth. You could emphasize this meaning by making the equal-armed cross a secondary symbol by placing a rose in the center to represent the spirit. You could then add more meaning by coloring the arms of the cross red, blue, yellow, and black to represent the four elements. The primary symbol is usually the most powerful because it has more potential to lead the mind in wider directions.

One of these symbols is a plain crucifix and the other is the Golden Dawn's rose cross. Look at each in Figure 1 for a minute, and then write down everything that occurs in your mind. The lists that you get might be totally different. For example, a study group given this exercise all said they received a more intellectual than spiritual information from the Golden Dawn cross, however, they felt that the purity of the plain cross provided more spiritual information than intellectual.

You can see your symbolic language in the seemingly anarchic visions of your dreams. Such dreams only make sense when you look at each composite symbol in the mold of your own experience. A dream where the cast of *The Sound of Music* came around to your house to sell you homemade jam would have to be pulled apart symbol by symbol. What does *The Sound of Music* mean to you? The film could be a symbol of heroes escaping from Nazi oppression. If you hate the film, it could be a symbol of mindless fantasy with an irritatingly catchy soundtrack. What did the jam represent? If you associate jam with long summer holidays and your mother making it, it could mean that your subconscious mind is advising you to relax. If jam represents calories and sweet things, then it could mean that you are having unconscious fantasies about fattening things.

Figure 1: A Crucifix and a Rose Cross

Other symbols called archetypes are common to most of humanity. These are and were "discovered" by the psychoanalyst Jung, who realized that some symbols in his patients' dreams had no personal meaning for the dreamer but still felt important.[6] Some symbols are common throughout human history, appearing in differing myths, religion, and creative writings. Jung reasoned that these common symbols were drawn from the Universal Mind, which he called the collective unconscious. These are the big symbols that seem to enter a person's mind just by virtue of the fact they are common to the experience of being human.

Every religion has an archetypal figure, whether it be Zeus, Isis, Jesus, Abraham, Moses, Buddha, or Allah. Myths and legends vary between cultures, yet they all seem to contain archetypal figures such as the Fool, the Seeker, the Maiden, the Crone, the Mother, the Father, and the Hero. These archetypes add weight to Plato's idea of an archetypal world dominated by primal ideas from which all other things proceed.

These very important primal images are vital for our well-being. Within our Inner Kingdom they can become distorted and effectively strangled by the complexes built by our life experiences. For example, there was one person I knew whose mother was a prostitute. When the mother would not want to have sex with her clients, she would send them to her underage daughter's bedroom instead. This so twisted the young girl's Mother archetype that instead of becoming one of nurturing care, the Mother archetype became one of fear and mistrust. The girl's biological father had long since disappeared, and so the only impression of the Father archetype came from her mother's pimp, who was the only stable man in her childhood, but the pimp also sexually molested the girl. The fact that these archetypal figures were so corrupted meant that all the pleasant things normally associated with parents were totally debased by distrust and fear. One of the key areas controlled by Mother and Father archetypes are relationships, because we tend to see the opposite sex through our initial impressions of our parents. As a result, this young woman's relationships with men and women were based on a mistaken belief that they would always betray her; this belief become a self-fulfilling prophecy. (We will look a little later at how we can begin to heal these archetypes.)

Changing Our Universe

It is an occult principle that as the universe is built from thought, it can be changed by thought. Thought can be used to enter to the deepest levels of consciousness (and to touch the very hub of the Universal Mind, diety itself). As an adept of the Esoteric Order of the Golden Dawn, Dr. Berridge once said you have to accept that your imagination has a reality. "When a person imagines he actually creates a form on the astral or even some higher plane and the form is as real and objective to intelligent beings on that plane as are earthly surroundings are to us."[7]

The method that occultists have used throughout the ages to bring about what they want is a very powerful technique called *visualization*. Put simply, visualization is to imagine what you want as clearly as possible, and to wish for it with every essence of your being. The latter is an important part of making what you want happen. According to Berridge, to change one's environment using magic, the magician must also ensoul the image in the mind with the will. Imagination can only create a finite image, which will fade over time. On its own, will, or simply the desire for something, can only create something that is vague and insubstantial. "However when the two are conjoined—when the imagination creates an image and the Will directs and uses that image, marvelous magical effects may be obtained."

By making a powerful image of what is wanted in your mind, and ensouling it with emotion and desire, it is possible to bring about your wishes. This principle has been a key principle behind the popular visualization movement of the 1970s. This movement was based around books with titles like *How To Get What You Want* and *How to Win Friends and Influence People*.

Visualization techniques expressed on these techniques are effective in most cases; many sales-training courses are based upon them. Essentially, these methods attempt to influence potential customers by visualizing the customers agreeing with the salesperson. Another technique involved a salesperson visualizing his or her commissions shooting through the roof or a customer leaving the shop with the product in hand. Other systems artificially enthuse the salesperson toward this goal, making the salesperson believe in his or her product so much that the sale's process is conducted with the same zeal as a Christian missionary trying to save a person from Hell by converting them. Such ideas activate the will so that the salesperson wishes to make the sale with all of his or her being. If this sincerity is achieved along with the appropriate visualization, then the sale is almost certain. Another sales technique worth mentioning is for the salesperson to get the customer to visualize himself or herself using that product. That way the customer starts the process of visualizing it for himself or herself.

The visualization movement flounders because while it can explain success, it has a greater difficulty explaining why it does not always work. There are many things that can prevent a visualization from having a desired effect. This is due mostly because when the new image is planted within your Inner Kingdom, it immediately has to fit within the framework of what is already there. Those things that fall short of the status quo are swiftly destroyed. This happens because your Inner Kingdom is the sum total of your past visualizations. If you do not believe in success, you have effectively crippled yourself from making new visualizations. The new visualization is like a seed cast on stony ground, and dies before its results can manifest.

Another issue is that you might get what you want, but it not may manifest in the way you wanted it. For example, you may have visualized yourself driving an expensive car as a symbol of you winning the lottery. After months of visualization, you receive a job that involves delivering such cars to wealthy lottery winners.

In the famous one-act play called *The Monkey's Paw,* a middle-aged couple are cursed with three wishes. They initially ask that they will save enough money to pay for their new house. Their wish is fulfilled when their beloved son is killed in a factory accident and they collect his insurance money. Distraught, the mother wishes for her son to be alive again, and when then they realize his mangled, rotting corpse has just crawled from the grave, they use their final wish to make him dead again. While never so dramatic, occultism is littered with similar stories of people getting things that they did not really want.

A magical school called Builders of the Adytum, of which I was a member, insists on the first page of its visualization course that people should not turn over the page before answering the question "What do you want?" At the time, despite my desperation to move on with the course, I could not really work out what I wanted. It was some weeks before I finally realized that what I wanted more than anything else at that moment was to turn the page and continue with the course. If you can answer the "What do I want?" question, the next one you need to work out is "Why?"

The answer to the "Why?" question usually indicates what you lack in your life. The thing you then have to ask yourself is whether acquiring this particular thing fulfills your wish. Visualizing the woman or man of your dreams sweeping you off your feet, for example, is probably one of the most pointless things to do, particularly if you have someone in mind, because what you are really lacking is love in your life, and what you want is to be more lovable to attract the right person. Generally, those people looking for a white knight (or lady), or the love of their life, are looking to escape any real surgery to their personality. They want someone to rescue them from their own Inner Kingdom rather than change it so that such a person can enter.

Having answered the "Why?" question, the next thing you need to work out is what are you prepared to do to assist your goal to manifest on the material level. There are many who visualize a good job for themselves, and then do not open the newspaper's employment ads, let alone go out and apply for a job. It is an absolute myth that money will magically appear out of nowhere with no effort on your part. Many magicians rarely perform magic to increase their income, not because they think it is unethical, but because the Universal Mind tends to give them more money-making work to do.

Below is a visualization technique worked successfully by many magicians in the Western Mystery Tradition. I suggest you practice it before you move on to the other exercises in this book. Try it with something small first, such as acquiring a book. The unconscious mind might actually work to prevent you from achieving a bigger goal, because it is tied up with previous behavior patterns. Most people's unconscious will permit small things to manifest, like books, though it is best to experiment with something that you are least likely to have personal blocks against its success.

A few successes will result in the system being adopted by your unconscious mind.

Basic Visualization

1. Sit in a chair. Make sure your arms and legs are not crossed, and relax as deeply as possible.

2. Think of a clear image of what you want. Build it as intensely as possible. Think of the color it is. If it is a physical thing, work out what it feels like, smells like, tastes like, or sounds like. Take your time over this stage because the clearer the image is, the more likely you are to get it to manifest.

3. Next, you have to stimulate your desire for the object. All else has to be put aside: at this moment all you can want is the object.

4. Visualize yourself as clearly as possible getting the object. Visualize a scene with you owning the object and then another with you owning the object in the past, as if you already possessed it.

If you followed the above technique to get a book, you would visualize the book's cover as clearly as possible. Feel your desire for the book. Then visualize opening it and reading a bookplate reading "This Book Belongs To _____" and your name on it. Then see yourself putting it on your bookshelf. Then think about the book as if it were already on your shelf.

If the visualization were something less tangible, like a new job, you would visualize yourself doing the job. (During job interviews, if I have decided that I want the job, I ask to be shown around the office. This enables me to get a clear picture of what it is like to work there for a visualization session later on.) You would empower that visualization with all the desire you can muster. Next, you would imagine yourself hearing on the phone that you had the job. Imagine how you feel about the news. Shut your eyes and imagine you are already working there.

The last stage is important in visualization because it anchors the visualization in the present, meaning that your mind does not get the chance to think of this as something for the future. (Remember, as far as your mind is concerned, the future never happens!)

The Five-Dollar Experiment

Once you have got the hang of the above exercise, I suggest you use it to see if you can get something tangible and material. The aim is to visualize yourself getting a five-dollar (or five-pound) bill within a month. The money must come from an unexpected source that is independent from your control. If you have mastered the technique, the money will come from an extremely unusual source. For example, a friend of mine used a similar technique, but the money did not arrive, even though he really needed it, until the last moment. He had practically given up on the idea when his cat brought in what he initially thought was the remains of a bird, but turned out to be a very dirty five-pound note. Others have reported finding their money lying on the sidewalk; one person was even given the money by a beggar!

The reason you are trying to visualize such a small denomination is that it will bypass any psychological blocks you might have that will stop you from getting the money. Many people suffer from a belief that they do not deserve to be wealthy and do not expect to become rich. However, even in such cases a person can visualize himself or herself getting a hold of such a small denomination without subconsciously blocking it.

From the Exhaustless Riches Exercise

This visualization is an expansion of the above exercise and its results are more significant. It is a variant on one taught to me by David Goddard many years ago, which I have tweaked to fit in with some of the psychological experiments detailed later in this book. Like the above exercise, it is designed to bypass some of the mental blocks a person might have to earning wealth (which could range from social conditioning to a lack of self-worth).

This exercise is based on the principle that the universe does not really want you to be poor. Deity is an infinite being, and "from the exhaustless riches of its limitless substance you can draw all things needful, both spiritual and material" (to quote a phrase from the occultist Paul Foster-Case in his "The Pattern on the Trestleboard"). There is a mistaken belief that somehow spiritual people need to be destitute because they have to forsake the material world. It comes from an old concept that this world was the domain of the Devil (or an evil creator god), which was severed from its omnipresent creator. This is an impossible contradiction. The divine being is omnipresent, it is everywhere, and for those of us who think all of creation, including money, is an internal expression of a loving deity, such ideas about self-enforced poverty are absurd.

It is nearly impossible to think about spiritual things while your tummy is growling and you don't know where your next meal is coming from. Even those monks who forsake the material world to live in a monastery get a few meals and their own hairshirt to wear. But for the rest of us living in the real world, it is a sign that we know what we are doing when we have enough cash or wealth to do most of what we want.

1. Sit in a chair. Make sure your arms and legs are not crossed and relax as deeply as possible.

2. Imagine yourself growing until you see the whole world at your feet.

3. Continue to grow until the sun is in your heart and the planets revolve around you.

4. See above you a barrier, it could be a brick wall, or a glass-like force field. This represents what is stopping the universe from giving you the wealth you want.

5. Desire with all your might the wealth of the infinite diety to rain down upon you. Know that this will happen if you let it.

6. When you are absolutely certain that you mean it, say out loud, "I allow myself to draw everything I need from the infinite source of all wealth, which is the divine being."

7. See the barrier shatter and golden coins rain down upon you, filling your aura.

8. Hold these symbols of material wealth to yourself and start to shrink down. As you do so, see the coins continuing to rain on you.

9. Shrink until you are your normal size. Look above you. The channel between you and the divine being is open and the golden coins are still pouring down.

10. Say to yourself, "From the exhaustless riches of the limitless substance of the divine being, I can take everything I need, for now and ever more. So mote it be!"

How Visualization Works

The universe is made up of spiritual matter that vibrates at different frequencies. The lowest frequency is matter, or the world we see around us, whereas the highest frequency is pure spirit. There are many different pitches that this energy works at, but it is essentially an expression of one thing working at different levels in much the same way that electricity works in a light bulb or a television. For simplicity, occultists grade this energy into four different levels or worlds. The first is Divine, the next is Archetypes, the next is the world of Formation, and finally there is the Material.[8] Occult teaching says that each world is influenced by the one above it and the ones below it. For example, an act on the World of Material would affect the World of Formation and vice versa. So if I wanted to make a change in my material existence, I would enter the World of Formation and place an image of what I wanted to happen ensouled with my will. This image would attract to it all the components needed in the World of Formation until it had enough structure to manifest in the next world.

The next level up is the World of Archetypes, which are what Plato called "forms." He believed that everything had an ideal version of itself that enabled us to identify what it was. Take, for example, a bed; each one is almost entirely different from another in color, shape, and size, yet we can identify it as a bed. That is because at the archetypal level there was a true bed form from which all others derived. It would have all the essence of "beddiness."

The essences at the World of Archetypes are extremely powerful and affect the World of Material by influencing the World of Formation. Normally, these archetypal figures have a clear rundown through the levels to the material plane through the World of Formation. This enables us to recognize the things we see and experience. Some archetypes have a rough ride as they pass through the World of Formation encountering the thinking and experiencing part of the personality that interprets them incorrectly. An example of this would be the girl I described earlier whose mother was a prostitute. In that situation, the Mother archetype would flow down the levels to the World of Formation where it would be met with the experience the woman had with her real mother. These feelings of mistrust, fear, and anger would block much of the positive side of the archetypal figure and only allow the negative sides.

Entering the Mind

Throughout this book you will be given techniques to explore the Inner Kingdom of the mind. But before that, we actually have to work out a way to get the Inner Kingdom. In fantasy novels, magicians visit magical kingdoms or other dimensions by waving a wand. At their command, a vortex forms and then they would step through into the other world just like a transporter in *Star Trek*. (In fact, there are some similarities between magical imagination and these particular fantasy images!)

In Western and Eastern magical systems, entering another reality involves some form of meditation, which shuts down the body, centering the mind, and switching consciousness from one level to another. This is achieved by relaxing as much as possible, regulating breathing until you get as close to possible to sleep (which is another time you enter an Inner Kingdom).

But relaxing is no easy thing in this stressful world; in fact there are countless experts charging businesspeople small fortunes for teaching relaxation techniques. Below is a standard technique that really works and will prepare you for deep meditation.

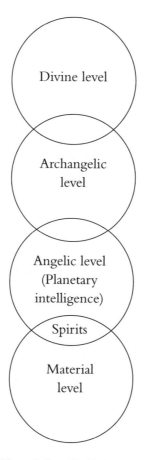

Figure 2: Four Worlds Diagram

Relaxation Technique

Sit in a straight-backed chair with your hands on your thighs. This is the position depicted in many Egyptian statues and is believed by some occultists to be showing someone performing a meditation.[9] Your back should be straight, your knees at right angles to the floor, and your legs uncrossed.

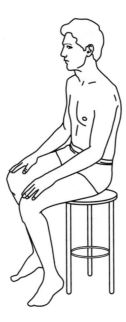

Figure 3: Meditation Pose

When you are comfortable, regulate your breathing. Breathe in and out as slowly and as deeply as you can. Say to yourself, "As I breathe out, all tension is leaving my body, and as I breathe in, I shall relax further."

Now think of every part of your body, starting with your feet. Say to yourself, "As I breathe out, any tenseness in my feet will leave, and as I breathe in, my feet shall relax." Repeat this until the feet are totally relaxed. Continue with the other parts of the body.

There will be some parts of the body that will be tenser than others and will require special attention, but the more effort you pay to relax them, the greater the rewards later in your meditation.

When you have completed your relaxation process (and this can take from fifteen to thirty minutes for the first few times) say to yourself, "I will now become more deeply relaxed."

Visualize an elevator[10] before you. You enter the elevator with the floors marked from ten down to one. You are on the tenth floor. Press the button marked "One," saying to yourself, "As this elevator descends, I will become more deeply relaxed." The elevator descends, and when it arrives you are at your most relaxed. Allow the doors to slide open, and you will find a plain wooden door before you. This is the entry point to your Inner Kingdom. Over the lintel is a symbol of protection. What that symbol is will be yours and yours alone. For now, just note what the symbol looks like, as it will be possible to use this symbol of protection in hours of need.

To leave this doorway to your Inner Kingdom, you only need to take the elevator. Say this to yourself, "As this elevator rises, I will become more aware of my physical body and surroundings." Step out of the elevator and see yourself as part of your own body.

The rest of this book contains powerful exercises. Before you attempt them, you should master the above process. After a while, you will be able to relax quickly and not need to use the visualization. Instead, you will just have to visualize the door.

Meditation

Meditation broadly describes the process of entering into an alternative state of consciousness. The two main types of meditation are called active and passive. Passive meditation is when you enter an altered state and images are allowed to enter the consciousness. Active meditation engages the intellect and tends to be directed. Active meditation is the most common magical technique taught in occult schools because it takes control of the thought process. Using a set of intellectually un-derstood symbols, active meditation guides the meditator along a par-ticular thought process toward a realization or spiritual goal.

Passive Meditation

Earlier I described how we develop association chains when we are growing up. Passive meditation uses this to find a root cause behind each symbol by mentally traveling down the association chain. If you started with a symbol such a cross, you would look at it until another idea entered your head . . . say an image of a hot cross bun. You would then follow that association, perhaps to Diana, the goddess of cross-roads and magic. By the time you have finished, you will have explored a whole network of associations in your mind.

Passive meditation is a tricky form of meditation because you shoot off at tangents and can get very lost in bizarre associations quickly. Using this technique, I once started out with a symbol of pentagram and ended up with a pot of blueberry jam, which contained very limited spiritual information. The trick is to push away associations that you know are going to take you away from your target. For example, when using the symbol of a white dove for peace, it would be good to follow the association with purity, but not a good idea to wander down the guano association.

Earlier, I gave an example of passive meditation on two different forms of crucifixes. Here are two more for you to try.

Passive Meditation Exercise I

Start with the elevator visualization and relax your mind as deeply as you can, regulating your breathing. When you get to the wooden door, see before you a circle with a dot in the middle. Ask yourself, "What does this mean?" Allow the door to open, and then allow images to ap-pear in the doorway.

Initially, you will see symbols that relate to intellectual information you have about circles and dots. Then, when you have exhausted this stream of information, wait, and after a while new information will arrive. Merge into the symbol so that you become it and it becomes a part of you. How do you feel? Allow more information to rise into your consciousness. Return to your body as before.

Passive Meditation Exercise II

This uses a chant of a divine name to have some form of mystical experience. Relax as before. Take a deep breath and chant the divine name IAO,[11] which is pronounced [Ee-ah-oh]. Breathe in and vibrate the name again. Repeat.

In these exercises you will get an effect that is uniquely your own. In some ways passive mediators are like someone who takes LSD in that they have no control over what they experience. Like many mystics, they may see the throne of the divine and experience great elation, unfortunately never repeating the experience because there was no ordered meditative method of approaching such a state. This is why active meditations are more commonly employed by magicians and occultists.

Active Meditation Symbols

Active meditation uses symbols to build a road of ideas to a particular spiritual idea or goal. These symbols are designed by people who have gone before and have obtained results by applying them in various combinations. Active meditation has the advantage over passive meditation in that although the problems of association chains remain, the mind can be steered away from heading down meditative blind alleys. The system's weakness is that its practitioners can become obsessed with the intellectual meaning of the symbols or become too reliant on symbols at the expense of spiritual progress that they are unable to drop them when the time for development comes. Sometimes a person might be led to a mystical experience in a pathworking but cannot abandon the symbol at the last minute to understand it fully. However, if an epiphany happens, active meditation users have a symbol to describe what they have experienced to others.

Active Meditation Exercise I

After your usual relaxation, choose one of the following sentences.

> The seed of Light
>
> All things are an expression of the One
>
> The kingdom of the divine is at hand
>
> Who am I?
>
> What do I want?
>
> Ruling the Inner Kingdom

Mull the sentence over in your mind until you understand it. Take each word and cut it apart with an intellectual knife, work out all its meanings, consult a dictionary if you have to. Remember that each word is a symbol and some of them are loaded with powerful archetypal meaning.

Next, relate each sentence to your life and then each word to other words in the sentence. See the sentence as a collection of symbols that are designed to teach you. Ask yourself, "What are the implications for the universe? How can I tie all this knowledge together?"

When you have run out of all the intellectual information related to this sentence, something new will happen, and suddenly the sentence, and the world, is seen in a completely different way.

This particular technique is wonderful if you are confused about how to approach a life crisis. Firstly, you have to convert your situation into a single sentence question, which is in itself a wonderful problem-focusing exercise. A seed idea is generally always positive, so it is not a good idea to choose the question "Why am I so useless?" The idea would be to find the seed of the problem in order to meditate upon it. For example, someone who has just ended another bad relationship could work out what he or she really wanted to know, and come up with something like "Why do I have bad relationships?" There are three keywords in this sentence that will generate interesting material, these are "I," "bad," and "relationships." After meditating on this one for a week, one person realized, much to her horror, that she chose bad relationships for the reason she did not believe that she deserved better. She also discovered that her definition of a relationship was wrong. Her mistake was she saw the romantic overtures of the relationship's beginning as a sign that there was a relationship, rather than simply a shallow, dramatic play for her affections by men who did not want to pursue anything more lasting. True, she had obtained romance, which was what she thought she wanted, but at the expense of a relationship, which she really did want.

Active Meditation Exercise II

Relax as normal and go to the doorway described at the end of the relaxation technique. Open it, and you will find yourself in sea of silvery mist.

After a while the mist clears and you find yourself in a cave.

In the center of the cave is a white stone, which fills the cave with light.

As you watch a stem of a plant grows out of the white stone, it buds and becomes a rose.

The rose opens and the cave is filled with its perfume.

In the center of the rose is a tiny golden child.

Bending over, you look at the child.

It looks at you with eyes of someone who has lived many times.

This is your Higher Self.

It grows and matures until it becomes a mirror image of you and raises its hand in a blessing.

You bow and depart through the door in which you came in.

Balance is Best

Sometimes I get asked which is the best form of meditation for those on a spiritual path of development. The truth is that both have their advantages and disadvantages. There are those that say that active is better for beginners who have yet to master the subtleties of inner vision, while others accuse active meditation of killing creativity.

Ideally, you should use a combination of both active and passive techniques. You should develop a system of symbols but just pause in an active meditation to just see what happens. For example, in Active Meditation Exercise II a passive element where you talk to your Higher Self could be added.

Using Imagination to Improve Your Memory

The first time we see the imagination being used in anything like modern pathworking is in memory systems developed to help poets and orators remember their speeches. These were codified during Greece's Golden Age by Simonides of Ceos (556 BCE–468 BCE). Although we are uncertain what Simonides actually invented, a third century BC tablet called the Parian Chronicle accredited him with inventing a system of memory aids. Roman writers Cicero, Quintilian, Pliny, and Ammianus Marcellinus back this up. We do know that all the ancient Greeks used a memory aid system that is uncannily close to modern pathworking. A fourth-century fragment known as Dialexeis can sum these up:

> If you pay attention you will be able to see things better.
> Repeat again what you hear, for by hearing and saying the
> same thing what you have learned is easier to remember.
> What you hear, place on what you know.

In other words, if you want to remember that Ajax was a soldier in the Trojan Wars, you could imagine him standing next to a statue of Mars in a room in your bathroom, cleaning the bathtub, with a big map of Greece in the background. So if you were going through a speech, you would mentally walk through your house until you got to the bathroom. In your mind's eye you could see a soldier cleaning the bath, remember Ajax,[12] see the map of Greece, and remember he was on the Greek side of the Trojan war.

Obviously this example is a little clumsy and the Greeks and Romans needed to codify things better to cover the long lists needed to remember their speeches. They already had a list of gods, who were attributed to the different planets. In memory terms all they had to do was see a statue of the god and then they would immediately think of the planet. Cronos (Saturn) would be a link to concepts like death, time, inheritance, and blackness, while Zeus (Jupiter) would connect to things like rulership, wealth, and purple. The net widened to include the zodiacal attributions. This meant that if they were making a speech about war with the Persians, they would use a magical image of a statue of Mars with the various points of their speech being placed around it in the zodiacal houses.

Here is another one developed by an occultist friend of mine, Elliot James, who used a memory system to give a tricky speech to his fellow American Civil War reenactors in the summer of 2001. He decided that his speech needed a number of quotations from the Articles of War (specifically Article 5—covering political speech by troops, and Article 54—covering behavior of troops in friendly territory).

He designed three rooms:

1. A hallway for his introductory remarks

2. A drawing room with French windows

3. A garden with a terrace

And then broke down his speech into various visual pictures.

For Article 5.

> "Any officer or soldier who shall use contemptuous or disrespectful words against the President of the United States, against the Vice-President thereof, against the Congress of the United States, or against the Chief Magistrate or Legislature of any of the United States, in which he may be quartered, if a commissioned officer shall be cashiered or otherwise punished as a court-martial shall direct; if a non-commissioned officer or soldier shall suffer such punishment as shall be inflicted upon him by a court-martial."

On the face of it, this would be difficult to memorize, but Elliot pictured himself moving into a room with French windows:

In the room was a table with a soldier's cap upon it—linking this idea to "Any officer or soldier who shall use contemptuous or disrespectful words . . ."

Then he saw a picture of George Washington:

". . . against the President of the United States."

Then a picture of John Adams:

". . . against the Vice-President thereof."

Then a snowshaker with a model of the Capitol on the desk:

" . . . against the Congress of the United States."

Then a picture a feather-boa (a trademark of Jesse Ventura, former governor of Minnesota);

". . . or against the Chief Magistrate."

Then a sculpture of a four-horsed chariot (as on the Capitol Building in St. Paul);

". . . or Legislature of any of the United States, in which he may be quartered."

Then he pictured a sword on the desk with the point toward him;

". . . if a commissioned officer shall be cashiered or otherwise punished as a court-martial shall direct."

Then a picture a row of chairs behind the desk;

". . . if a non-commissioned officer or soldier shall suffer such punishment as shall be inflicted upon him by a court-martial."

Having finished that part of the speech, Elliot moved to the French windows, opened them up, and then moved on to the next part of his speech.

There was a side effect of using this memory system: people using it started to pick up "new" information about their subject. This side effect was noted and explained by the philosophers Plato and Aristotle. Both considered obtaining knowledge as simply recovering information (remembering) that had been forgotten when we were born and fell from our perfected state in the higher realms of existence. So when people were using these memory systems it was no surprise that they "remembered" something else about the subject at the same time.

It was perfectly reasonable that memory systems could be used to bring new information to the conscious mind of the practitioner. This is important because by contemplating esoteric symbols, you can unlock secrets of the universe that have been hidden within them.

In the Middle Ages and later, memory systems were developed, particularly among Renaissance magicians. One of the great researchers into memory systems, Frances A. Yates, suggests in her book *Art of Memory*[13] that these classical techniques have evolved into the medieval magical system called the Ars Notoria. Under this system, she says, the magician would stare at magical symbols, recite a prayer, and gain knowledge of all arts and sciences. Each Ars Notoria memory picture was allocated to a branch of knowledge such as philosophy, metaphysics, geometry, mathematics, or theology. A person would look at a picture dedicated to philosophy and say the following prayer:

> "Gezemothon, Oronathian, Heyatha, Aygyay, Lethasihel, Iaexhizliet, Gerohay, Geromay, Sanoaesorel, Sanasathel, Gissiomo, Hatel, Segomasay, Azomathon, Helomathon, Gerochor, Hojazay, Samin, Heliel, Sanihelyel, Siloth, Sileech, Garamathal, Gese, Atal, Gecoromay, Gecoronay, Samyel, Samihahel, Hesemyel, Sedolamax, Secothamay, Samya, Rabiathos, Avinosch, Annas, Amen."

Then the following prayer:

> "Oh Eternal King, Oh God, the Judge and discerner of all things, knower of good sciences; instruct me this day for thy

Holy Name's sake, and by these Holy Sacraments and purify my understanding that thy knowledge may enter my
inward parts as dew falling from Heaven and as Oil into my
bones. By Thee Oh God Saviour of all things who art the
fountain of goodness and origin of piety. Instruct me this
day in those holy sciences that I desire. Thou who art One
God forever. Amen."

Then the knowledge would slowly filter its way into his or her conscious mind, either during a dream or just as a flash of understanding.

It is not clear how effective these systems were, but we know they
were used by many medieval people because of the large number of
copies of Ars Notoria that have found their way into the many different museums over the years. For this number of copies to have sur-
vived means that they were the medieval equivalent of a bestseller.

Close to these memory glyphs are those pentacles found in the famous magical text, *The Key of Solomon*. These pentacles were geometric symbols, usually painted on wooden disks that were held in the
hands of magician when they called a spirit as part of a magical rite.
However, I know a number of magicians who have received insights or
"memories" when staring at these symbols. This could be because the
pentacles held links to the spirits behind them or might have the same
effect as the squiggly lines of the Ars Notoria. More research needs to
be done into the use of such pentacles in this manner by experienced
magicians. There were several pentacles attached to each planet with
different spirits attached to each pentacle, and some of these spirits
were not very nice.

Planetary Images

There were more obvious images associated with memory that were
not only more widely circulated, but also give us a safer method of remembering the things we want, and gaining new insights. These mem-

ory pictures of the Middle Ages give us archetypal figures for each of the planets that can provide the sort of information you want.

Below, you will find seven planetary image descriptions that were designed by the sixteenth-century magician Cornelius Agrippa to have the maximum possible impact on your unconscious mind and allow you to understand the planetary forces. Some of the images are familiar; others will strike you as strange. This is because they were in the language of the unconscious, and the unconscious mind can produce some strange and disturbing images at times!

If you want to remember something, make a story out of the magical image that includes what you want to remember. If you want to remember that the password on your computer is "Badger," you would place a badger on Mercury's lap,[14] perhaps with the word "password" written on it. If you have a problem with your computer and are trying to find the solution without bothering the help desk, you would visualize this magical image and ask it for help.

Which Planetary Image Do You Use?

Saturn

Fate, time, the past, limits and boundaries, form, structures including houses, old age, ambition, bones, knees, skeleton, shins, ankles and circulation, rheumatism, arthritis, envy, suffering, feat, guilt, toxins, repressed aspects of the self, death, vermin and lice, politicians, scientists, architects, teachers, mines, mountains, and wastelands.

Jupiter

Lawmaking, opportunity, growth, progress, evolution, money, banks, rulers, royalty, faith, hope, charity, redemption, freedom, spiritual wisdom and development, hypocrisy, hips, thighs, feet, lawyers, priests, counselors, actors, open spaces, public places, and panoramic views.

Mars

Wars, anger, action, sexual desire, physical energy, guards, courts, justice, courage, protection, transformation, revenge, destruction, surgery, the head, genitals, excretory system, rashes, red spots, migraine, predators, soldiers, surgeons, athletes, furnaces, furnaces, and metal work.

Venus

Love, eroticism, desire, pleasure, inspiration, joy, partnerships, peace, friendship, creativity, the arts, beauty, evaluation, promiscuity, overindulgence, lewdness, gentle animals, the throat and neck, kidneys, lower neck, diplomacy, artist, fashions, bedrooms, and gardens.

Mercury

Communication, movement, messengers, computers, the media, language, trade, theft, magic, skill, learning, intellect psychology as a science, science, rationality, cunning and mischievous animals like monkeys, digestive system, arms and hands, merchants, clerks, accountants, scholars, universities, examinations, shops, schools, airports, and train and bus stations.

Moon

The unconscious, habits, instinct, sea, rhythm, the astral realm, mysteries, women (particularly their health), mothers, childbirth, psychics, menstruation, mental health, the stomach, breasts, warts, sterility, obsessions, delusions, insanity, cleaners, brewers, midwives, sailors, and harbors.

The Sun

Leadership, general health, healing, organization, arrogance, display, drama, fathers, power, individualization, the heart, the back, the lungs, kings, directors, managers, actors, palaces, and theaters.

The Planetary Magical Images

Saturn

An old man dressed in black, sitting on a high chair, his hands are above his head, and he holds either a fish or a sickle. Under his feet are a bunch of grapes and his head is covered with a black cloth.

Jupiter

A crowned man dressed in saffron-covered robes riding an eagle or a dragon. In his right band is a dart, and he is about to strike the eagle or dragon. Or, a crowned naked man, who has his hands joined together and lifted up. He is sitting in a four-legged chair, which is carried by four winged boys. Or, a man with the head of a lion, or ram and eagle's feet, clothed in saffron-colored robes.

Mars

An armed man riding on a lion, carrying a naked sword in his right hand and a decapitated head in his left. Or, a soldier crowned, armed with a long lance.

Sun

A crowned king clothed in saffron colors, sitting on a chair, holding a raven, with a globe under his feet. Or, a woman crowned with fire, dancing and laughing while standing on a four-horsed chariot. In her right hand is a mirror, or shield in her left. Leaning on her breast is a staff.

Venus

A woman with the head of a bird and the feet of an eagle, holding a dart in her hand. Or, a naked young woman with her hair spread out, holding a mirror. There is a chain about her neck, and a handsome young man holds the chain with his left hand as he fixes her hair with his right hand. They look lovingly at each other, and a winged boy holding a sword or dart is about them.

Mercury

A handsome, bearded young man. In his left hand is a caduceus, and in his right is a dart or a flute. He has winged feet. Or, a man sitting in a chair or riding on a peacock. He has eagle's feet and a crest on his head. In his left hand he holds a rooster or fire.

Moon

A man leaning on a staff, with a bird on his head and a flourishing tree before him. A horned woman riding a bull, a dragon with seven heads, or a crab. She has in her right hand a dart, and in her left a mirror. She is clothed in white or green and has on her head two snakes with horns joined together.

A word of caution here. Just because the magical image gives you an answer does not mean that it is right or that you heard it correctly. Sometimes (particularly when you ask a magical image about your love life) your lower unconscious mind will put the words it wants to hear in the magical image's mouth. For example, when I had a crush on a woman and wanted to know if she was interested in me, I approached the magical image of Venus and asked it if the woman was interested in me. I was told emphatically "Yes!" but I noticed that the image actually shook her head when she said yes (in other words, the image was saying no but my lower self was blotting this out). Confused, I asked again and this time the head nodded while the voice said "Yes." All that had happened was my lower self had realized that the image was shaking its head and made sure it could not do this again.

When using magical images it is always important to listen, watch, and accept that the first thing you were told was the proper message. Then test what you have heard against logic and reason. It is possible that you have been conned by your lower self, so you have to be careful. My first reading of the situation was correct. The woman was not interested, and the magical image had told me so.

CHAPTER TWO

Modern Magical Imagination

Magical schools continue to develop the use of magical images and symbols as methods of training. Most of these schools, like mystical secret societies, implant a set of symbols within the minds of their initiates during initiation rituals. The advantage of performing a ritual is that the ritual exposes a person to a dramatic presentation of a symbol and the effect that it will have on that person's life. The candidate would study these symbols as part of his or her training within the school until the candidate could walk the symbolic paths depicted by these rituals. An example of this is the Freemason system, where a candidate is presented with a set of symbols and allegories during an initiation ritual. The symbols are those of a worker building Solomon's temple, and by mediation and use of this allegory the candidate is expected to become a better Freemason and person.

In the eighteenth century, magical schools started to develop another mind technique based on the idea of a journey through an inner landscape, or through a myth where the practitioner was the central character. Usually these journeys were carried out in the rarefied setting of a magical ritual, which gave the journey more impact. One Napoleonic-period ritual manuscript shows the candidate identified with the myth of a page heading toward King Arthur's court.[1] During the page's journey (which is read aloud by one of the officers in the ritual), the candidate/page has several adventures. After each one, the page is rewarded with the knowledge and control of the elements of fire, earth, water, and air. By the time the ritual sequence of the candidate/page is completed, he or she arrives in King Arthur's court, where the candidate/page encounters more adventures. The climax of the ritual is the candidate/page being finally knighted (a symbolic integration of the soul and the body).

In the late nineteenth century, this technique developed into something called "traveling in the spirit" or "rising through the planes." Although this sounds flowery, this magical imagination technique is essentially where a person in deep relaxation visualizes himself or herself undergoing various experiences. Perhaps one of the greatest exponents of this technique was a magical order called the Esoteric Order of the Golden Dawn.[2]

The Golden Dawn

Founded in 1888 by Freemasons, the Esoteric Order of the Golden Dawn was pivotal to the way magical imagination material was developed for nearly a hundred years. The Golden Dawn influenced many magical groups that have used its techniques. For this reason, it is worthwhile looking at some of the teachings of the Golden Dawn in regards to magical imagination.

The order's basic technique involves sitting in a chair, relaxing and regulating your breath, and then visualizing yourself ascending upward toward the divine being. This was called "rising through the planes" or "spirit travel." This technique also made it possible to enter into a tarot card, or any other mystical symbol using this technique.

According to a Golden Dawn Instruction Paper,[3] the adept should:

> Proceed to the contemplation of some object, say a Tarot
> Trump: either placing it before you and gazing at it until
> you seem to see into it; or by placing it upon your forehead
> or elsewhere and keeping your eyes closed. In the last case
> you should have given previous study to the card, as to its
> symbolism, coloring analogies etc.
>
> In either case, you should then deeply sink into the ab-
> stract ideal of the card, being entirely indifferent to your sur-
> roundings. If the mind wonders to anything disconnected
> with the card, no beginner will see anything spiritually. You
> must then consider the symbolism of the tarot card, then all
> that is implied by its letters, number, and situation. . . .
>
> The vision may begin by the concentration, passing into
> a state of reverie or with a distinct sense of change (some-
> thing allied to the sensation of fainting, with a feeling urging
> you to resist). If you are inspired, fear not, do not resist, let
> yourself go and then a vision may pass over you).[4]

This same manuscript gives a detailed example where one of the
order's chiefs, S. L. MacGregor Mathers, and an adept, Elaine Simpson,
entered into the tarot card the Empress. They found themselves in a
pale-green landscape with a gothic temple.

"Here," wrote Mathers, "there appeared a woman of heroic propor-
tions, clothed in green with a jewelled girdle, a crown of stars upon her
head, in her hand a sceptre of gold. . . . She smiled and said: 'I am the
Mighty Mother Isis . . . I am she who fights not, but is always victorious. I am that sleeping beauty whom men have sought for all time.
Such who fail find me asleep. When my secret is told it is the secret of
the Holy Grail.'" This secret turned out to be the heart of nature, the
love that runs behind and supports everything.[5]

Later in the life of the Golden Dawn, one of its adepts, Florence Farr, developed an organization within the Golden Dawn called the Sphere Group. This group was designed to work solely with magical imagination techniques with the aim of "turning evil into good." Although the Sphere Group featured many different journeys during its work, the organization's central operating method was to get participants to visualize spheres of divine energy around the immediate vicinity, globe, solar system, and universe.

The main inner work of the Golden Dawn used a Christianized version of the Jewish mystical system of the Cabbalah as a roadmap of consciousness. This was based around a diagram called the Tree of Life, which showed ten aspects of God connected by thirty-two paths. The meaning of the diagram is complex, because the diagram can be read as both a roadmap for the evolution of a human, or a description of God itself. The ten stations have ten aspects of God: the Crown, Wisdom, Understanding, Mercy, Severity, Beauty, Love, Splendor, Foundation of the Creation, and finally the Kingdom. Since Cabbalah (and the Bible) say that humanity is made in God's image, these stations have a correspondence within each of us. The Kingdom is our physical body; the Foundation is our unconscious mind; Splendor is our intellect; Love is our higher emotions, and Beauty our spiritual self. The other spheres are more abstract aspects of ourselves. Severity is the way we destroy; Mercy is the way we build. Then we have within us the creator God and Goddess (Wisdom and Understanding), which are divisions of the One Thing (the Crown).

These stations on the Tree of Life are linked by thirty-two paths, which were agencies that make up these spheres. The paths were considered important by the Golden Dawn because each one represented a Hebrew letter, a tarot trump, a planet or zodiacal sign, an archangel and angel, and certain other symbols. The Golden Dawn believed that by traveling along these paths in your mind's eye, you would come to understand the deep meaning of the symbols and unlock the keys to

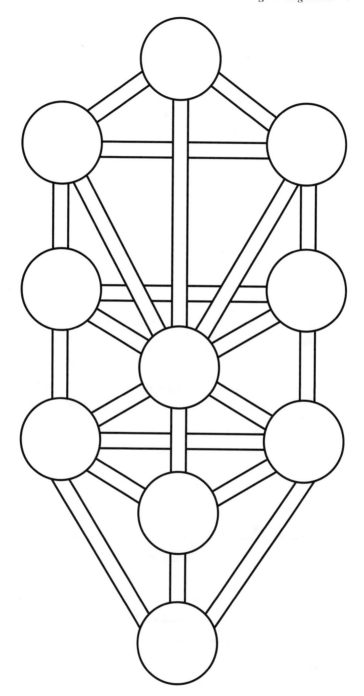

Figure 4: Tree of Life

the spheres, the result of which would be mastery of yourself and then mastery of the universe. Later, magicians who used the Golden Dawn techniques called traveling along these paths *pathworking.*

The method for ascending these paths involves visualizing a door with the symbol upon it. The adepts would step through the doorway and into an imagined landscape. During the Golden Dawn's elaborate system of initiations, adepts were given passwords and signs so these codes would be fused into their unconscious mind. Any beings the pathworking adepts met on the other side would be tested using the Golden Dawn's many grade signs and passwords, to make sure that a malicious spirit was not deceiving them. If the spirit did not reply with the correct password, the adepts knew that either the spirit was mischievous or they had not attained the right state of consciousness. For example, a Golden Dawn initiate encountered a being who gave a password that indicated it was a water entity. But the initiate believed that he had pathworked into a fiery element. Since water was considered "below" fire in the pathworking this initiate was attempting, it was clear he still had a way to go to get to the proper state of mind needed.

Halfway through the journey a symbol appears that would give an indication that it was time for the adept to come back. The journey would always end when the adept stepped out of the doorway back into this time and space.

Below is an example of a Golden Dawn pathworking for you to try. It is along the path of Tau and leads to the lunar aspects of sphere of the Foundation. Since it has been designed for those who are not Golden Dawn initiates, it is impossible to "test" the visions that you see with the grade signs and passwords as any Golden Dawn initiate would do. If you would like to try some more Golden Dawn pathworkings, I suggest the *Self-Initiation into the Golden Dawn Tradition* by Chic and Tabatha Cicero, and *The Tree of Life* by Israel Regardie. The tarot card used in this pathworking is the Universe card, and is from the *Golden Dawn Tarot Deck* designed by Tabatha Cicero. I recommend you see this card in its full-color glory to have the best effect.

Figure 5: Universe Card from the **Golden Dawn Tarot Deck**

Journey to the Moon—A Golden Dawn Pathworking

After you have relaxed and regulated your breathing, visualize a doorway before you. On the lintel of the door is a Hebrew letter ת. Over the doorframe is a violet curtain with a picture of the tarot card, the Universe. Take your time to visualize this scene as clearly as possible, soaking up the symbols until they seem to take on a life of their own.

Step into the curtain and you find yourself in a sea of silver mist.

This mist slowly clears and you find yourself looking at the mouth of a cave. In your hand is a lantern. Instead of candlelight in the lantern, there is a Hebrew letter ת, and it glows with a cold blue light.

You enter the cave and find yourself going along a passage that is getting slowly narrower, until the passage becomes an entrance, about which are carved the images of a bull, an eagle, a man, and a lion.

You step through the door and into a cavern. In the center is a dancing hermaphrodite who holds two wands. The hermaphrodite radiates a light that sends shadows dancing in tune inside the cave. The hermaphrodite then vanishes, but leaves the ghostly outline of the Hebrew letter ת in the air.

You walk along the cavern until you come to a dark underground river. There is a boat here, and a boatman looks at you with cold eyes. "Only the dead may pass over the river Styx," he says with a voice like the grave. "By what token do you seek passage?"

You draw in the air the Hebrew letter ת, and he motions for you to get onto his boat. "He who has hung on the cross of the elements may pass both ways through the gates of death." Without another word, the boatman rows you across the river to a beach. You get on a beach, then go into the mouth of another cave. This cave winds upward, but the cave's ceiling is low, and you have to crawl on your hands and knees. Sometimes you feel that you will become stuck, but somehow, with some scrapes, you end up emerging into another cavern.

You hear the rushing of the ocean in this new cavern, and the air smells of saltwater. You walk out of the cavern and onto a sandy beach. Soft hazy creatures of light move around you and you see that the beach is full of them. They are watching the full moon rising. You hear on a wind their gentle voices almost whispering "GABRIEL."

Then, as the moon sends a silvery pathway across the sea, you become aware of a bright light coming toward you. Unlike the other creatures, this light has substance and power. It has the head of a beautiful woman, with an alabaster face and blue hair. She has a slim body from which blue and white wings beat. In her right hand she holds a silver chalice, and in her left hand a wand with two snakes curled about it. Around her feet walks a lion.

Her power is overwhelming, almost knocking you to your feet. The wispy creatures[6] move through the air, hoping to touch this being, but she approaches you, speaking. What does she say to you?

After Gabriel has spoken, you ask her for a vision of the divine aspects of the moon, of the foundation of the universe.

"Look into the moon, Son (or Daughter) of Man, and pray that Shaddai El Chai shall appear in his glory."

You look into the moon and wait. Then something happens. What happens is up to you.

When the vision has departed, you find yourself back at the cavern where you saw the dancing figure. You retrace your steps through the cave and back out the doorway. Turn and you see the tarot card on the door fade into a purple light. You then slowly become aware of this time and this reality.

Modern Developments

Those magical groups that followed in the Golden Dawn's footsteps almost universally adopted the order's pathworking techniques. Perhaps the most significant was the Society of the Inner Light, founded by Golden Dawn initiate Violet Firth, who is better known by her pseudonym Dion Fortune. Fortune made many of the Golden Dawn's teachings more accessible to her students, allowing them, for example, to take place in a pathworking to the Inner Temple of the Order before a ritual took place. This enabled those taking part in her society's rituals to work on a physical and an inner level at the same time. Something similar to a pathworking was performed before a Golden Dawn ritual, but only by a select few senior adepts in the temple.

Fortune was greatly enamored by the almost spiritualist practice of establishing contacts with inner plane beings whom she met while using similar techniques to pathworking. It must be said that the Inner Light followed the Golden Dawn's formula and, as far as I am aware, still do. It took one of the Inner Light's best students, the writer Gareth

Knight, to start seriously tinkering with the Golden Dawn's system of pathworking during the 1960s.

Knight wondered what would happen if you used the standard pathworking technique but focused on different symbols or legends. This was a time when another former Inner Light student, the writer William Grey, was also experimenting along similar lines.[7] Some of Knight's students and associates included Marian Green and Bob Stewart. This led to an explosion of experiments among the esoteric groups in the UK, and mirrored a change in occult groups towards less rigid structures. The techniques developed between these people resulted in a dramatic change in way in which we do pathworking.

A pathworking now became an exploration of an inner world. A guide would take a group or individual on a journey to explore that particular region of inner space. Some of the results could be interpreted in psychological terms, while others clearly gained something spiritual, but nothing that required much in the way of structure, other than knowledge of symbols on the part of the guide or teacher.

The work in the UK was mirrored by some non–occult research in the United States, carried out by the Foundation for Mind Research. During this period, the Foundation was looking at the creative process and exploring trance states. The result was the development of systems that occultists would call pathworkings, and in some respects was a more scientific re-inventing of the wheel. Drs. Robert Masters and Jean Houston published much of the material in 1972 under the title *Mind Games.* This book had a series of pathworkings that had the same goals and techniques of many occult groups.

Pathworking had now become a key part in the training of occultists in the UK. When W. E. Butler wrote a five-year correspondence course for his school, the Servants of the Light, he based the course entirely on an inner landscape using the Arthurian myth. Using pathworking techniques, Butler was able to have his students prepare for higher magic by training them in an inner landscape and unconsciously opening the gates for the energies Butler wished to be activated to make them ready for initiation.[8] We will be looking at a similar concept to Butler's in the next chapter.

By the 1980s, pathworking became commonplace in the UK thanks to the writings and workshops of Marian Green and Dolores Ashcroft-Nowicki. Ashcroft-Nowicki's *Shining Paths* was a modern take on the old Golden Dawn system, using Hebrew letters to ascend the Tree of Life. Its structure was far looser by the time she wrote another series of pathworkings titled *Inner Landscapes on Tarot Cards* a few years later, where the inner journeys were completely fluid and more inspired by the card rather than a structure of pathworking. Pathworking techniques within her school now meant a journey to a particular inner plane temple or location, and often included a meeting with a spiritual being.

Below is a more modern pathworking to try, which is based on a journey to read the Akashic Records. Occultists believe that nothing is forgotten, and that every life in its minute detail is recorded forever within the Universal Mind in the Akashic Records. If it is possible to tap into that universal memory, a person could understand all history from the standpoint of someone that was actually there. The Akashic Records works as a sort of telepathy across time. Many branches of occultism have a belief that we have lived many lives before, and sometimes it is possible to remember them. This pathworking will help you find images of your past lives to explore. I should point out that while this pathworking may not actually find you a real past life, it may just give you an image of another time and place and enable you to see the world through another person's mind. Whatever your experience, there will be a reason and logic to the viewed past life. "The Universal Library of Consciousness" pathworking might provide you, in symbolic form, an indication where your current life is going. I personally think that 99.9 percent of past-life memories are simply this. Too many claim to be priests and priestesses of various gods—one person I know was adamant that she guided the fleets of Atlantis to the shores of Britain. But like the magician W. E. Butler once said, "I have never met someone who has claimed to be an ancient Egyptian dustman."

The Universal Library of Consciousness Pathworking

Open your inner eyes. Before you is a revolving door that turns slowly clockwise. On the right hand of the door, on a brass plate, are the words "Universal Library of Consciousness"; beneath this is written "Open All Hours."

You enter the revolving door and find yourself in a large corridor, which has a heavy desk at the end of it. Above the desk in imposing letters is the word "Inquiries," and beneath this sign is an unimposing man with small, round glasses and a wispy, white beard. He is carefully covering a book in plastic so that it will survive the rigors of life on the shelves, and the man is doing his task with such concentration and precision that he hardly notices you approach.

You clear your throat and he looks up, peering over the top of his metal-rimmed glasses.

"Yes?" he says in a tone mirrored by countless librarians throughout the ages. "Can I help you?" His tone suggests such disinterest in your actual reply and an obvious hope that you will go away.

"I would like to have a look at a certain book please," you tell him. "It is an autobiography on my life."

"Is the book finished?"

"Finished?"

"Are you dead yet?" he asks in his imperious tone.

"No."

"Then go the 'Living Reading Room,' sit down at a counter, type your name and date of birth into the computer, and your autobiography will appear in the slot beside you. One volume for each incarnation you may in the 'Living Reading Room' request for any former incarnations. Return the book by placing it back into the slot." This sentence is delivered as if it had been the same for centuries, with each initial letter emphasized for effect. He directs you to a double door, through which you step and find yourself in a corridor.

On your left is a sign that says "Living Reading Room" and on the right "Catalog of Former Incarnations, History (Civilizations Current), History (Civilizations Expired), Mammal Wing, Fish Wing, Lizard Wing, Plant Wing, Insect Wing, Organic Matter Wing."

Of course, you think, *everything from a human to a stone has a memory and this must be recorded in this place.* You walk down the corridor until you come to a double door with a sign above it, which says "Living Reading Room." You open it and find yourself in a huge, circular room. At the room's center is a massive, circular computer bank, from which lines of desks emerge like spokes of a wheel. Above the reading room desk is a huge dome, on which is depicted the sun.

Hunched over the reading room desks are countless people of different races and religions, all reading from different books. Their eyes are glazed over, as if they are not really here at all but have been transported to another place and time by the words they are reading. Occasionally someone will blink, shut the book, and look thoughtful. People come here instinctively when they seek to discover something about themselves by evaluating their past. They do not, of course, need the symbol of the library to get to the information.

You sit at a desk. In front of you are a computer screen and a keyboard. There is a slot on the right-hand side, like one used for mail. On the screen, in large friendly letters, is the phrase "What Name Do You Want To Access?" You type your full name. After that, the screen reads, "What Date of Birth?" You type in the information in. At the "Which Place?" prompt, you type in the location and hit the Enter button.

The screen goes blank except for the cursor . . .

Then the computer prints out your name, address, date of birth, time of birth, and asks you if this information is correct. If it isn't, type "No," and the computer will search again. (This occasionally happens if you have a common name.) When you have the correct name, type "Yes." On the computer screen there appears a message: "Book of Life Found And Being Delivered." You hear a whirring noise of conveyer belts, and, after a while, a large black book is poked through the slot by unseen machinery.

On the book's cover is your name, and on the spine is a number and name, which is not yours. The name on the spine is the secret name of your Higher Self, and the number is the amount of times you have incarnated. Deep in the stack room of the library there is a long shelf with a line of books with this Higher Self's name upon them, and this book you are holding is the latest volume.

You turn to the back of the book and open it. Words are appearing as you look. You shut the book, and then turn it over to the front. There is a big picture of your birth, but seen through your eyes. As you look at the picture, your eyes begin to glaze over, and suddenly you are remembering the whole birthing incident. You can remember the light, the confusion, the pain of the cold air . . . *everything.*

You squeeze your eyes shut, and you are holding the book in the library again. *Right,* you think. *I am going to open this book at random and find a memory in my past, which I need now to understand something that I am going through.*

You open the book at random. There is some text but there is also a picture of a scene. You look at the scene and experience it.

When you have finished this scene, you shut your eyes, open them again, and you find yourself back in the library. Now it is time to find out about your past lives. You note the number and name on the spine of the book and return it in the slot. On the computer screen there appears the message "Do You Want Another Search?" You type "Yes."

On the screen appears the phrase "What Memory Do You Want To Access?" You type the name that appeared on the spine.

A message appears on the screen. "That Is A Soul Name. Is That Correct?"

You type "Yes," and the computer asks you for a number. This is the number that appeared on the spine. If you want to know about your last life, you would type the number less one. (For example, if the number for this incarnation was 34, you would type "33.")

When the book arrives, it will tell your name, date of birth, and details of your life and death. Each incident in that life will have an illustration, which you can enter by simply staring at it.

Experiment for a while and learn. Think about this past life that you have experienced. How relevant is it to the life you are living now? What did this person do right that you can learn from, and what did they do wrong that you too are experiencing in your life? Carry these lessons in your heart and meditate hard on them. When you have finished, return your book and leave the library the way you came.

The Perils of Pathworking

There is a certain amount of danger in pathworking because it is a form of willed disassociation, and some psyches cannot deal with too much of it. Some people suffer from mental illnesses, of which disassociation is a symptom and, therefore, there is the danger that they might disappear into the imaginary realms and not return.

Pathworking can be addictive, particularly for those whose lives are not that pleasant. For these people, they can ascend into pathworking as a means of escape from their world, rather than an attempt to change it.

In the late 1970s, a role-playing game called *Dungeons and Dragons* was developed by TSR, and the game gained a huge amount of popularity in the 1980s. This game would be controlled by a person taking on the role of Dungeon Master, who would describe what was happening, while the players, role-playing as a character in a fantasy setting, would then respond what they would do in response to what the Dungeon Master informs them. As the game progressed, the imaginations of the players would be expanded until they started to get as excited as if the game was really happening. The more imaginative the Dungeon Master and his players, the more real the game would become, so much so, that if the player's character died, the player might have an emotional response far above that which would be expected for a simple game.

As the *Dungeons and Dragons* game became more elaborate, some players wanted to remain in the character of the heroes that they were role-playing in their games. They looked at their lives and decided that *Dungeons and Dragons* was better than the real world, so they retreated into the game, some living just for the game. These escapists became trapped into the framework of a game, and reality had become meaningless (which is a pity, because *Dungeons and Dragons* is harmless and quite useful at enhancing the imagination).

Dungeons and Dragons uses the same sorts of techniques as modern pathworking, even though the game is not conducted in the deep altered states. Although *Dungeons and Dragons* was only used by a small number of people in a negative way, it should be remembered that the same result is possible with pathworking, which is littered with more powerful symbols. Here, the addiction is not gained through winning treasure or rescuing a princess, the lure is based on the spiritual release that the use of such symbols can provide. It is possible to forget that the goal of pathworking is to bring about change, and not to simply write and perform it for its own sake. This is why I always suggest that each pathworking should have a goal to bring about change in the material world.

You should not do more than one pathworking a week when you first start. More experienced people can managed one every three days. However good and experienced you are at pathworking, you need three days simply to process what you have experienced. The exceptions to this are workshops where people have to pack in a certain amount of experience into a short space of time. In such workshops, as many as five or six pathworkings can be packed into a weekend, leaving teachers and students a little burned-out by the experience. Some teachers limit any negative effect by talking about the results of such pathworkings in some detail to help the person ground the experience. I also recommend that people do not do any pathworking for at least ten days after such an intensive session in order to give the pathworkings a chance to have an effect.

Different Types of Pathworking

There are two main forms of pathworking: passive and directed. A passive pathworking is when you are given the barest outline of a scene and leave the person taking part to see what he or she wants to see. Although it is largely uncontrolled, passive pathworking is good for allowing access to a person's unconscious, which allows aspects of a person's higher mind to communicate with the lower personality. A passive pathworking would have extremely general instructions such as "Visualize the god Anubis speaking to you," but the rest of the pathworking is left to the spontaneous imagination of the person. It is from passive pathworking that a person receives inspiration and new material.

During a directed pathworking, everything is controlled to achieve a specific effect on the unconscious mind of the pathworker. Directed pathworkings must be designed with a goal (for example, an understanding of cosmic love) and be littered with specific symbols to allow that aim to be achieved.

An effective pathworking contains elements of both passive and directed methods. A more controlled pathworking might take a person through a series of symbols to meet a guide. Then a period of passive meditation might take place, where the guide gives specific information unique for the person who is taking part in the pathworking. The person is then guided back to this reality as the pathworking becomes more controlled.

There is a third, rarer form of pathworking that is unique to magical groups. This is when a group of people is taken to a place on the astral plane using directed methods, and then, once they have arrived, each group member describes what they see until a collective picture is built up. What is unusual about this method is that after a while everyone sees the collective scene so clearly that the effect has a tremendous impact.

Below is an example of a transcript of exploring a particular inner realm connected to the element of earth, by three magicians whom I will call A, B, and C. After the group leader had taken them though a door by a directed method, they were left in an image of silvery mist. Once this mist cleared, the trio collectively built up the scene.

A: It is cold.

C: I am standing on shingle rock.

A: I am getting that too.

B: I can see that the sky is black, but I don't think it is night.

A: Yes, it is hard to imagine any stars in that sort of blackness.

C: There is vegetation; it looks like dark cactus.

B: Yes, I can see them, they look like the tall Cactus Jacks you see in the desert.

C: I have just tried to touch one and it has split into four. It is hollow and full of something like gas . . .

The story continued until the met one of the beings of this place——an angel.

C: He spells his name Z A Th B E L[9]

B: So he is a Hebrew angel.

A: He has a cube in his hands. Ask him what he does!

B: He says he is a catalyst and his job is to speed up chemical reactions.

A: So how can we use him?

C: He does not understand . . . I don't think he is something that can be called upon . . . he is just a force within nature. . . .

A: In the rock itself, yes. What are the cacti then?

C: Zathbel does not see cacti . . . he sees . . . I am picking up a word like "insubstantial symbol."

A: The cacti are a symbol to us, but to Zathbel they have a different meaning?

C: Yes, that is it! They are a symbol that the densest matter is really not as solid as it looks.

A: Zathbel is nodding.

B: Yes, I can see that too. He is saying that once the element of earth is examined closely, it is as insubstantial as air.

This conversation went for many exhausting hours before everyone got tired and decided to return. The result for this group was that they had the name of an angel they could use if they wanted to speed up a magical reaction. What was interesting about this pathworking was that it was to a specific part of the Earth, which was identified later as being Serbia. This was several years before trouble in the former Yugoslavian republics boiled over into war and ethnic cleansing.

Pathworking and Astral Projection

It is easy to confuse pathworking and astral projection. When you astral project, your body is left behind with just enough of your consciousness to keep your body functioning. Your disembodied consciousness floats within an astral shell through the various levels of creation, which are still shaped by the mind of the astral projector, and so the consciousness encounters creatures and a landscape, but there is a feeling of reality. One important way that this landscape differs is that the colors and feelings are intensified. It is possible for an intelligence to be a color or a geometric shape. The strangest thing is that whatever you want to happen, or wherever you want to go, you will be there almost instantly.

There are those who believe that when they are doing pathworkings at a deep level and lose awareness of their physical bodies, they are actually astral projecting. Unfortunately, this is only partly true. A pathworking, however deep, is a vision of the astral with your mind's eye, and it is not the same as taking your entire "self" there for a look. It is a bit like watching a movie in which you might feel that you are part of the scene, but you only have to blink, or hear the person in front of you scrunching a potato chip bag to be returned to reality. No one watching a movie about cowboys in the American Old West would say that they have astral projected to Tombstone however deeply they were absorbed with the movie. If you astral projected into a movie, you would be like the person in Woody Allen's film *The Purple Rose of Cairo,* interacting with the characters and changing the plot.

The similarities between pathworking and astral projection mean that the former is training for the latter. The first time I astral projected I was completely disorientated, however, I suddenly remembered all the pathworkings that I had performed over the years and could control the experience of astral projection. Pathworking techniques give you all the information you need for a safe astral projection; the only difference is that you do not leave your body.

Writing Your Own Pathworking

On the surface, constructing a pathworking is like writing a short story or novel. In conventional writing, you are most likely to have a beginning, a middle, and an end; it has characters, a setting, a plot, and a theme. Unless a pathworking is simply going to be reading a work of fiction to a bunch of very relaxed listeners, it has to be a little more than that.

At the heart of every pathworking is a magical objective, which might be to understand the nature of the element of fire, or to understand why a person is frightened of spiders or lacks self-confidence. The "plot" of the pathworking is based around that particular objective. The philosopher Plato wanted to explain the fairly complex concept that our reality was simply a shadow of a deeper truth, and he used an allegory, which if it were turned into a pathworking, would look something like this.

Plato's Cave Pathworking

Imagine you are a prisoner in a cave, chained, facing a wall. You are chained about your neck so that you cannot move your head to the right or left. All you can see is a small amount of wall in front of you. There is a fire behind you, and it casts flickering shadows on the wall. You are aware of other prisoners chained in the cave, but because you cannot see them, conversation between you soon dries up. All you can focus upon are the shadows on the wall in front of you. Soon these shadows become a means to escape; they take on a life of their own and you are swept away in your imagination with these dancing figures. The occasional cry from the other prisoners indicates to you that they have found the same thing.

Years pass, and your mind has taken on the belief that the shadows are all that there is, short of the disorientating moments when food is thrust into your mouth by your jailer. In those shadows, your life plays out in a flickering, gray show.

Then suddenly one day you are unchained and lead out of the cave. As you pass the fire, you see that the fire created the shadows that had been the focus of your life for so long. Then, as you are led blinking out into the sunlight, you see the world is bright and full of color lit by the sun.

You bask in the glory of that which you had forgotten over the years. Here is a real light, real color, and real life. After a while, you start to think of the other prisoners in the cave, chained to their shadows without a hope of the light that you now see. You rush back into the cave to tell them what life is like outside. One by one they tell you to go away. "Our lives are these shadows," they say, "we have much invested in them." Not only do the prisoners not believe you about your "tales" of light and color, but they also do not want to hear the truth.

Allow the scene to fade.

In the above example, the entire plot is centered on trying to make the pathworker understand the central theme. Once that happens at this deep level, this revelation will have a considerable impact on the pathworker. This pathworking will have bypassed the conscious reasoning of the person and allow him or her to see the central theme in a totally new light.

The other important element of a pathworking is the use of symbols. Scenes within a pathworking should be built around a central archetypal symbol that reacts with the person's unconscious. This adds considerable psychological power to the pathworking and helps to raise the pathworking's intensity. In the above example, the central symbols were chains and shadows. These two objects sent a symbolic message to the unconscious that the pathworker is bound to a false reality.

Meetings with gods, goddesses, hermits, wise people, and animals in a pathworking are all steps along the way toward unlocking particular aspects of the unconscious and building up an emotional and spiritual effect. These symbols do not have to be in the pathworking's center stage; you could make the pathworker walk alongside a fast flowing river in which salmon are swimming upstream. There need be no explanation of this particular symbol in a pathworking, as the unconscious mind will pick up the symbol and act upon it. It understands that the salmon, which is a symbol of wisdom, is going against the flow of the river, which symbolizes the mass mind. Such a symbol would be important if you had designed a pathworking to help someone break free from conventions that were keeping him or her chained to the shadows.

Knowledge of what these symbols mean takes some experience, which is why beginners rarely write pathworkings. If you meditate on symbols, their meanings will become apparent over time. Fairly obvious ones are easy to uncover; these are the archetypal figures such as Mother, Father, Wise Person, Fool, and Trickster. The meanings of animals can be found within the shamanic tradition. *The Druid Animal Oracle: Working with the Sacred Animals of the Druid Tradition* by Philip Carr-Gomm could be a good introduction for animal symbolism. The elements of fire, air, water, and earth can provide powerful symbols for a pathworking.

1. **Fire:** Energy, power, destruction, transmutation, illumination, the sun, the father, conception, wisdom

2. **Water:** Compassion, understanding, mutation, the moon, prophecy, the mother, the unconscious, gestation.

3. **Air:** Communication, healing, intellect, mind, speed, Mercury, the son, growth

4. **Earth:** resources both natural and material, sleep, the planet Earth, cold, darkness, the daughter, death.

Having read the list above, you should be able to tell what would happen if you wrote a pathworking with a magical well of prophecy, which is activated by plunging a torch into its waters!

Writing a Pathworking

Words are symbolic guides in a pathworking. Words should be written with care so that they do not lead you from the atmosphere you are trying to create. In some books on pathworking, you might find writers saying that it is important to use clever language and poetry, usually lifted from writers like Blake, Coleridge, or Yeats. The logic is that the evocative language used by great writers and poets may inspire the reader to achieve great heights in a pathworking. I disagree. While it is true that words are symbols and the likes of Yeats knew what they were doing when it came to using them, the use of another's words in a pathworking you are writing is at best lazy (and a little pretentious), and at worst outright dangerous. A poet, like the writer of a pathworking, is trying to use words for a specific purpose. Although the poem might say it is about joy, the words that the poet is using are actually pointing to a moment in his or her life. This is fine if you are reading the poet's work, but using those same words will lead your pathworkers down the same route. Hijacking the poet's purpose is a bit like using a hammer to drive in screws—it might work but you are more likely to end up with a lopsided set of shelves.

The same applies to lifting whole tracts of sacred and religious verse. Sacred texts are usually written in a different era and a different language, and lose much in translation. It is not that the words are wrong, but these texts will lead your pathworkers to an ancient place that is alien to their modern minds. The religion of ancient Egypt was never the religious utopia that many New Agers would like to believe. The various gods and goddesses all have their dark sides; even the beautiful mistress of magic, Isis, has her sinister aspects. It is impossible to know what I am going to access if I incorporate what seems to be a beautiful evocation to Isis from the Pyramid Texts into a pathworking.

It is possible to use these sorts of prewritten text in pathworking; we just have to adapt them using our own modern minds and symbolism. If I had written a pathworking where the person meets the crocodile god Sobk, I could quote the Utterance 317 from the Pyramid Texts and end up with something like this:

> I have come from out of the waters of the flood. I am Sobk, green of the plume, watchful of face, raised of brow, the raging one who came forth from the shank and tail of the Great One who is in the sunshine.

> I have come to the waterways which are in the bank of the
> flood of the great inundation to the place of contentment,
> green of fields, which is in the horizon that I may make
> green the herbage which is on the banks of the horizon,
> that I may bring greenness to the eye of the Great One
> who dwells in the field.[10]

On the face of it, this passage is an evocative piece of writing that would look good in a pathworking. But even the translator R. O. Faulkner had to guess about what parts of the passage means. Faulkner assumed that since the "Great One" is described using feminine words, it is probably a reference to one of the great goddesses like Neth. The upshot is that if I use this in its ancient (even translated) form, I may get more than I bargained for. So I have to work out what I really want this god to say so that it sounds similar but is still in keeping with this pathworking's direction. I have to use my symbols and my words to make this happen. Since the theme of the pathworking in this case is "beauty in nature," I could rewrite Utterance 317 until it becomes:

> I am Sobk who comes forth from the sacred waters of the
> Nile.
> Watchful am I,
> Still am I.
> I am the Raging One who was born from the sky goddess
> Who holds the sun.
> I come with the blessings of the gods on the sacred land.
> I stand on the land so that it may be fertile and green.
> I bring a beautiful vision of nature to the Great Goddess
> As she watches over us.

It is not the same text, but it has been inspired by the original and retains some of its flavor. But my passage as written has anchored symbols I will not go anywhere I don't want it.

When writing a pathworking, words should be used sparingly. It is vital that the imagination of the pathworkers is allowed to blossom in the pathworking. It is the rogue elements that you do not put into your script that make the pathworking personal and magical. If you drown the pathworkers' imagination in a sea of prose, the pathworkers become lazy and don't have to use their imagination. This means that these unchallenged pathworkers will not have the chance to really use their inner eyes and pick up new and exciting symbols. One of the most frustrating books I ever had to study in school was John Steinbeck's *The Pearl*, because everything in it was described in so much detail. It seemed to me that, although I could see things with my imagination, Steinbeck insisted on describing everything to me, including lots of information that I did not need or want to see. If a hero walked across a yard, it was unnecessary for me to have to sit through a long description of what a chicken was doing in the corner of the imaginative picture. This would just be distracting from the goal of the pathworking.

Keep your descriptions as brief as possible, and sentences short. If a teacup is blue, don't call it a frail, eggshell, turquoise teacup with dark-blue vine leaves upon it. Unless the symbols of the vine leaves are important, the teacup should remain a "blue teacup" and nothing else. The phrase "You are in a dark forest" will be enough without describing the meandering of snake-like vines and sinister trees that look like ancient bearded men. There are exceptions to this rule. If you want to make a point in a pathworking, use a suddenly dramatic descriptive word that is packed full of meaningful symbolic words. For example:

> You are in a dark forest.
> You have the feeling that you are being watched.
> Pressing down the pathway you come to a clearing.
> In the center are the remains of a burned-out fire.
> This place smells of fear and the trees look as if they have been tortured.

The last sentence is designed to give the pathworker a sense of dread. Notice that it does not say, "The trees were twisted, broken, and bent like they had been tortured." You have left that point to the pathworker's imagination.

The other place where you can "go to town" with your language is in the speech of the characters your pathworker will meet. This is because the language should give the pathworker a sense of the character's being. Normal people do not speak in short sentences, but they don't often use long and colorful words either, and to put such language into their mouths does not make for a plausible conversation. In a Norse pathworking, a peasant should say, "It is raining so heavily out there that you can hear the old Odin's hammer in the hills," and not, "This precipitation lashes like a cat-of-nine tails against the windows of our fair lodge. Harken, doth that not be the hammer of ancient Odin crashing and rumbling against the gray stone mountains as he furies against the ice giants?" You might want to give your characters an accent or use words that are out of date to give a pathworking a historical feel. One of my teachers loved to have his angels use plenty of Old Testament-style language with the argument that the unconscious understood and responded to the ancient language better. This was, he said, because the unconscious was an old part of the human psyche and understood old language. I beg to differ. The English language may look the same in print as it did 400 years ago, but the words were spelled and pronounced very differently from modern English. For example, the word "nun" was pronounced as "noon." Shakespeare's English would have sounded like West Country English, only with so thick an accent that it would be very hard to understand. In my view, it is better that modern languages are used and that the pathworkers understand it.

A pathworking should not last longer than twenty minutes. This is about the maximum time a mind can stand without slipping into sleep or starting to feel uncomfortable. Almost 90 percent of what you write that happens after this time will be lost. If what you want to achieve cannot be written in a twenty-minute pathworking, then break up the pathworking up into twenty-minute sessions, with pauses for discussions between. After about thirty minutes of pausing, the mind will be rested enough to go on. However, be careful here, for although the mind does see the same pathworking as a solitary action, a series of pathworkings lasting many hours requires the endurance of marathon runner. One "all-day" pathworking I took part in once left me feeling so spaced out it took me a couple of days to recover.

A pathworking should always end where it began, and pathworkings usually starts at a door. Convention says that the door should look like the historical period in which you are entering. If you were writing a pathworking with an Egyptian theme, you would use a door in the style of ancient Egypt, with a winged sun disk on the lintel; a Celtic door would be two sacred trees or even a cromlech. The reason for this is that the period doorway enables the person to unconsciously re-orientate himself or herself afterward and trains the unconscious mind to always return to the place it left. This is particularly useful if a person later develops his or her astral projection skills.

You should also include phrases at the beginning of the pathworking that give the pathworkers a chance to enter an altered state. This would be a period that allows people to relax and regulate their breathing. You should try to make the pathworkers as confident and relaxed as possible about what they are about to do. Reassure them that if they feel frightened, they only have to say a word and they will return to the doorway through which they entered the pathworking. You should also suggest to them that throughout the pathworking they will always hear the sound of your voice. This is important, because if they lose the ability to hear you, they will find the trip back harder.

You should also write an ending to the pathworking that enables the person to become fully "grounded" afterward. My favorite is a ritual formula that I learned from one of my teachers, which I have adapted over the years. After the pathworkers have returned through the doorway, I say:

> You are a creature of spirit manifesting in the material world.
>
> Feel the elemental vehicle in which you travel upon the Earth.
>
> Feel the heat in your body—this is fire.
>
> Feel the air in your lungs—this is air.
>
> Feel the water in your mouth—this is water
>
> Feel the weight of your bones and flesh—this is earth.
>
> You are a creature of the four elements and spirits.
>
> Open your eyes, stamp your feet, for you dwell in Earth again.

Narrating the Pathworking

Narrating the pathworking is harder than it appears. Generally, pathworking sessions, whether passive or directed, have one leader who guides the pathworking person or group through a particular sequence or narrative properly. The leader's role is not just to read a story to a group of pathworkers, but also guiding a group of people through a mystical realm. The leader needs to be able to read the story while at the same time "see" in his or her mind's eye what is happening. People in a pathworking do stray off from the goal time to time, and it is important that if you see this, you work out a way to get them back to the group's goal.

Group leaders have to be wide awake on the Earth level to look after the people in their fragile altered state. If anything happens, the guide has to be able to bring the pathworkers back quickly, but if the pathworkers come back too fast, they could find themselves at best disorientated or, at worst, in a state of psychic shock.

Group leaders should also endeavor to experience the pathworking themselves to ensure that they receive the benefits of the particular pathworking they will lead. This requires a sort of split-level working, where the group leader ascends and descends often. After a workshop or a day's worth of pathworking, I am usually very tired because of the hard effort that this sort of activity takes.

The pathworking should be read slowly, with long pauses between each sentence. This allows the pathworkers a chance to "see" what is being described to them, and incorporate any new things that have not been written into the pathworking. This also takes a bit of a knack to get right, because although a pause may seem a long time for the person reading it, it may seem very fast for the people experiencing the pathworking. This problem is eliminated if the reader is accompanying the pathworkers taking the journey.

After a pathworking is complete, the group leader should discuss the pathworking with each person in the group. This process is to help the individuals to remember their experience. This recall is important, as pathworkings are a little like dreams in that they are forgotten very easily if they are not written down or discussed quickly. This also gives the group of pathworkers the chance to discover similarities between what they saw. One of the strange things about group pathworkings is that people do see the same things, even when these items are not scripted into the pathworking. There are often slight variations, sometimes in color or shape, but often these differences are due to the person's inner symbolic language. One person might see red as a color for excitement, while another might see it as a color for violence. If these same two people saw an angel of excitement wearing a tabard, one will see the tabard as red while the other will see it as yellow.

One thing you will notice is that some group members might feel that they have fallen asleep during the pathworking. They typically say they "lost" the thread of the pathworking at a certain point. This was a cause for concern for me as a group leader, and I used to watch these people closely during a pathworking. To my surprise, despite their complaints that they feel asleep, they were usually with the group throughout the pathworking and they always "woke up" when the pathworking was finished. It was occult teacher Marian Green who came up with the answer to this problem as a result of research with her many students. She believed that rather than "losing it," the path-workers had slipped into a deep level of consciousness, so deep in fact they had lost the use of their short-term memory. They were experiencing the pathworking but they could not remember details of it. Her answer was to discuss what happened with them after the point her students thought they had "lost" consciousness. Sure enough, it was possible for them to piece together what they had missed. Even if they could not remember the pathworking at a certain point, if they woke up with the others then the full effect of the pathworking had pervaded into their unconscious.

There are exceptions to this occurrence, as sometimes people do fall asleep during pathworkings. They tend to snore or don't wake up when the pathworking has finished. Sometimes their heads fall forward and the pathworkers wake up with a start. Such people need to develop better concentration skills and also make sure that they get enough sleep before they perform the pathworking.[11]

Sometimes there are those who always fall asleep and there might be a medical condition that needs to be explored. One American occult teacher, who had a problem with one of her students nodding off all the time, accompanied him to the doctor for a blood test, and the student discovered he was coming down with the early signs of diabetes. When the student underwent treatment, he was able to stay awake.

Unusual Things That Can Happen to a Pathworker

There are a number of physical side effects that happen to a person when he or she is in deep meditation or taking part in a pathworking.

None of these conditions are harmful, particularly if you know what is happening.

Paralysis

This is when the person for some reason becomes aware of his or her body during a pathworking or meditation, and focuses on the body. However, the awareness is only partial and most of the person's consciousness is still taking part in the meditation or pathworking, and so it is hard to rouse the highly relaxed body. To the momentary returning consciousness, the body feels like it is paralyzed and cannot move. This sometimes creates a moment of panic, causing the pathworker to return to full consciousness and fully rouse the body. This sometimes occurs naturally during sleep and is nothing to worry about. In fact, in some Eastern systems of magic, yogis train for months to achieve a really good state of paralysis.

Pain, Itches, and Twitches

This is very common, particularly among inexperienced meditators or pathworkers. Although sometimes these sensations are caused by the person not sitting correctly, it is more often due to the lower aspects of the personality attempting to assert itself. The lower self feels threatened by the pathworking, because it knows that the exercises will bring about change. The lower self is fairly inert and likes things to stay the same so that it does not have to think too much. What changes occur to the lower self, it generates pain or, more commonly, an itch, which forces the person to scratch himself or herself, causing the consciousness to come out of a deep pathworking. The first few times this happens it is important not to give in to these minor signals. Giving in to an itch may spoil the pathworking, and you should ignore it. Eventually, the lower self will give up on that tack if it knows you are determined to ignore the discomforts the lower self generates.

Sensation of Body Slumping Over or Moving

The first time this happened to me was when I was hypnotized and it is a strange sensation. I was convinced that my head had slumped onto my shoulders. I could feel it there, and in the vision that I was required to have I felt as if I was watching the vision with my head cocked to the left. After the session was over, I remarked to the hypnotist that the session had been spoiled because my head had moved and I was too relaxed to bring it back up again. He seemed surprised, as my head had not moved at all and I was sitting bolt upright throughout the session. Much later I discovered that this is common among people who are in a deep altered state. Their consciousness slips out of the body and becomes free from it. This is part of the early stages of astral projection. If the person is unaware of what is happening, the freed consciousness stays put or slumps. This happens more frequently with people for whom astral projection is achieved easily.

Seeing Things

This happens when a person is not properly grounded after a pathworking. They see shapes, darting images, or other people's auras. This is because they are so used to seeing with inner vision that when the pathworkers return they still use it. This might seem like fun (and in some pathworkings it is a good idea to get people to open their eyes so that they can see their surroundings with inner vision), but usually seeing with inner vision is disorientating, and if someone is attempting to drive afterward, downright dangerous. A good hot drink and something to eat generally sorts that problem out. Sometimes physical activity also can help with the grounding and shutting down of the inner vision.

CHAPTER THREE

Building Your Own Inner Kingdom

The best way to learn about Inner Kingdoms is to build one and explore it. This chapter will show you how to do that, and give you a taste of a system of meditation, which, if you wish, could be the basis of your meditation patterns for the rest of your life. It could also give you the inspiration to build one that closely responds to your own personality. The Inner Kingdom uses some of the active techniques we examined in the previous chapter, but has a significant passive pathworking element. There is much that you will need to discover and build for yourself; however, the aim of this chapter is to create the framework for self-discovery. I have included more structured pathworkings within each section of the Inner Kingdom so that you can see how the Inner Kingdom operates, but you will get much more out of this pathworking when you start to plan your own Inner Kingdom. Your personal Inner Kingdom is a living and breathing creature of your imagination, which is more personally powerful than any tangible artwork you might create. In fact, many artists would say that their art is only a shadow of their imagination.

Earlier, I described a door to your Inner Kingdom, and the question was left open as to what you would see on the other side. Generally, that exploration is up to you. The rawest picture of your Inner Kingdom is the chaos of your dream state. However, there is some evidence among occult schools that if you accept a standardized glyph of an Inner Kingdom, it is possible to slowly reshape your unconscious. When maps of these Inner Kingdoms are drawn, these layouts often become elaborate symbolic diagrams or mandalas.

The esoteric school Servants of the Light (SOL) used the Arthurian landscape for its mandala and focused on a castle layout, which represented the physical and psychological body of the operator. Locked in the basement of the castle were those prisoners or complexes that you did not want to deal with, and at the top of the castle was your spiritual self. One exercise involved walking around the castle's medieval village of Camelot with the goal of interacting with the wider part of the unconscious—the part that is shared with other people. Still further away from the castle were parts that belonged to others, many of whom were spiritual beings. It was possible in this exercise to see oneself in relationship to the rest of the spiritual and material universe by using this layout as a template for understanding.

Because all of these places were seen through the glass of your imagination and colored by personality, some of the visions have to be interpreted symbolically. For example, one magician was shocked when she saw the people of Camelot having a bearbaiting contest in the middle of the town square. It would be tempting to see this as an example of the evil that is contained in humanity, that which tortures animals. Since she was the "king" of Camelot, she was in a position could make a change, perhaps issuing an edict banning bearbaiting, and then such cruelty would be outlawed. The effect is that the "law change" would go some way to limit cruelty to animals. However, it is more likely that the bearbaiting means something more personal to the person viewing it, and many have walked through that particular Inner Kingdom without seeing the bearbaiting. It was probably a psychological image that she could work out using her own symbolic language and the legend of King Arthur as a reference.[1] Perhaps she believed that the world was against her and would tear her to bits if she trusted another person. The name "Arthur" was probably derived from the name of the Celtic god Artor (meaning "the Bear"), and in the SOL mandala the pathworker took the role of King Arthur, and so it is possible to interpret the bearbaiting image as the pathworker's belief that people were ready to torture "her."

The Arthurian world is a good design because it merges the pagan and Christian worlds, and is loaded full of archetypal symbolism. As king, you are in charge of your Inner Kingdom and responsible for it.

There are other mandalas that can be used either from a historical epoch or from your or someone else's imagination. Material from fantasy, historic, or science-fiction books can provide good landscapes, so if you are a *Lord of the Rings*, *Star Trek*, or C. S. Lewis fan, this ready set of mandalas gives you the opportunity to incorporate the symbols that moved you into your own Inner Kingdom. I know of one person whose Inner Kingdom was centered on an office with him as the chairman of a company. Another person built a science-fiction *Logan's Run*-style dome, complete with laser defense systems. There was another who was an English Civil War reenactment buff who built a fortress with musketeers, pikemen, cannon, and cavalry.[2]

Below is a fairly simple map of an Inner Kingdom called the Hall of the Hero. Not only will the Hall of the Hero give you some ideas to play with, but also it is complete and has been tested to see that the symbols work. It is based on a Celtic mythos, but could have easily be adapted to medieval, Arthurian, or the ancient Rome, Greece, Egyptian, or Atlantian worlds. Remember that this world has a reality of its own with a unique time and space, but this makes it no less real than the physical world outside.

To visit this kingdom in pathworking, I recommend you study the diagram first, and then record the description or have someone else read it to you, making sure that each sentence is read slowly and there is a pause after each sentence. This pacing gives you time to imagine what you see. You will only need to do a directed journey once to make sure that you know where everything is and build the basic structure. Thereafter, you can visit and rely on your memory of what you saw the first time.

Take note in a diary of everything you noticed in the Hall of the Hero that is not described in this pathworking.

To enter this kingdom, use the relaxation exercise to journey to the wooden door, and let the door swing open into silver-colored mist. Step into the mist, which slowly clears to reveal the following scene.[3]

The Hall of the Hero

As the mist clears, you are looking at a roaring fire; the smoke is rising upward toward a hole in the thatched ceiling. Surrounding the fire are roughly cut tables and chairs. There is freshly straw on the floor. You are in a large chamber. Behind you is a long table, with a large chair in the center. This is your chair.

You are the chieftain.

On the table is a sword. It is a broad slashing sword with two serpents for a crossguard. It is your sword. With it, you rule your tribe and your territory. On the right of your big chair is the chair for the bard, and on the left is the chair for your partner.[4]

Around the walls are shields, and there are three doors on your right and three on your left. Behind you is a large doorway, which leads to a courtyard with a well. The courtyard is enclosed by a stockade, which encloses the hall. Beside the well is a stepladder that leads to a tall watchtower.

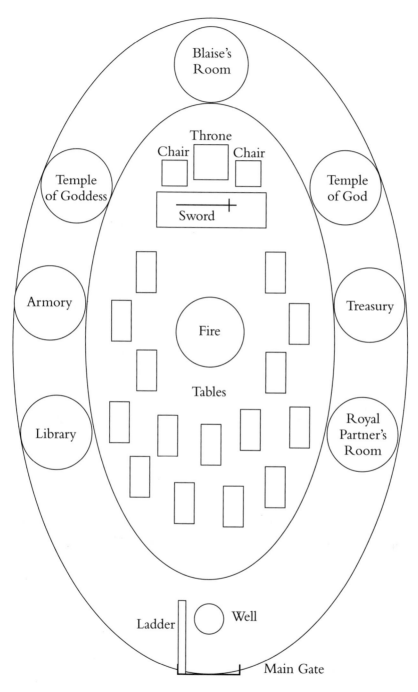

Figure 6: Hall of the Hero

You are a mighty Celtic chieftain. Your hall is large and has seven chambers. The first one, closest to the door on the left as you enter, is a library where scrolls of knowledge are kept. The door on your right as you enter is where your partner sleeps. It is a room dedicated to love.

The next door on your left is the armory, which is full of weapons and armor. Traditionally, this room is where you would try the tribe's criminals when they have broken the law, and also arm the tribe for battle against the enemies of the kingdom.

The next door on your right is the treasury, where you keep the laws of land. You go in there if you want to change an unjust law or to distribute treasure to the tribe, either as a reward or if they are in need.

Slightly behind the throne on the left is the room dedicated to the Mother Goddess. Slightly behind the throne on the right is a room dedicated to the Father God.

The door behind the throne is where the bard Blaise sleeps and composes his magic. You are indeed fortunate, for your tribe is a host to the greatest magician and bard in the land. Blaise taught the legendary Merlin the Enchanter, and it is Blaise who is your guide and helps you arrive at the best decisions for your land. Sometimes he gives you advice that is wrong, not out of malice, but because it is important that you test all his advice and know how to stand on your own two feet. So you must weigh his advice carefully. No one goes into Blaise's room, for the ground is considered even more holy than the temple of the God and Goddess.

As you walk out of the hall, you are in a small courtyard with a well. Some say the well is magical, and many people enter the courtyard to deposit small coins into it for luck. The courtyard is surrounded by a stout stockade and there is a gateway into the village outside.

Notice in which room you sleep, as it will say a lot about your orientation. If you sleep in the library, you might be more logically and rational-thinking orientated; in the armory, you could be defensive or aggressive; and selecting either the Goddess or God room could indicate a paternalist or materialistic phase in your life. You will also notice that where you sleep will change. Try to think why these changes might be happening.

Notice the colors of the clothes that the inhabitants wear. Try to see what these people represent to you.

The well outside represents your unconscious. In times of stress, its waters will seem troubled; other times you will be able to use the well's waters to see into the future.

When you are experiencing a period of conflict in your life, the armory door will be open with different types of weapons or armor made ready. These could tell you the best way to deal with the problem. If the sword is there, it means that you will have to close and fight with your adversaries. A spear would mean that you will have to fight, fending off your opponents but not becoming too closely involved. A bow means you have to keep your distance and strike from afar. If there are no weapons, or the door to the treasury is open, then you must not fight and must either be kind or forgiving. If neither door is open, there is no action for you to take at this time.

People who enter the hall are almost universally aspects of your personality. This is particularly true of the warriors who you will find populating your hall. The arrogant warrior who sows discord among the others and insists on making conflict is a part of you, and you must find a method of bringing him or her into line. This process of externalizing your personality traits is a powerful way of finding out about yourself. Your role as a chieftain is to bring peace to your hall, and sometimes it is going to mean banging some heads together, other times it is going to require some skilful diplomacy.

One example would be if one of the warriors comes to you, complaining that another has stolen his or her horse. On the surface, this would seem to be a traditional gripe in a Celtic society and was normally dealt with by a trial by combat. In your role as a chieftain, however, you have to assess what this symbolically means. The warrior who is making the complaint might represent how you relate to your partner. The accused warrior who has "stolen" the horse, a symbol of power, could be a representation of your work. In other words, you are working too hard and allocating too much power to your work, hence your relationship is suffering. It might be in your interests for the "work" warrior to keep the horse for now, and the "relationship" warrior to be compensated.

Always check to see how the warriors respond to your decisions. While you might have the final say, your job must be to make sure that all sides are happy and the tribe, which is your overall personality, is not put out by the decision. For example, if the "relationship" warrior still remains unhappy, this could mean that the compensation you are proposing is not enough. It is an unconscious warning that your partner is about to get angry about the way he or she is being treated, and your relationship will not survive unless it gets its balance back fast.

Sometimes it is impossible to please the whole tribe, even with the most sensible decision, and this is because you are destroying a complex or a pattern of behavior that is entrenched in your psyche. In most cases, if you look closely at what you are changing, you will find out what the cause of the problem is and you might have to really work at forcing the warriors to obey your ruling.

Besides receiving a warning from your unconscious that your relationship might be heading toward trouble, this imaginary conflict has shown you the best way to handle it. You can take counsel with Blaise (who represents your spiritual self) over some of the trickier decisions.

Remember: Things that change in your hall will gradually change in your own personality.

Feast Days

You can use the Hall of the Hero to hold imaginary feast days, inviting your warriors to meet with other beings to learn more about the land.

These feasts have to be conducted carefully, as you are allowing beings that are not necessarily part of yourself into the center of your imaginary kingdom. The best way to do this is ask Blaise to visit the surrounding lands and invite beings whom he thinks the kingdom would benefit from meeting. Blaise will bring warriors, priests, peasants, doctors, and so on, one at a time into your hall. You should receive them politely and sit them beside you, listen to what they say, and reflect on what they tell you. Always make a ceremony of thanks and farewell and see them leave. Each feast should be a single meditation session, and if a stranger outstays their welcome, your warriors and Blaise should escort them from the building. Blaise will usually step in and threaten to satirize the wrongdoer in every hall in the land if the being does not leave, and this threat will motivate any into leaving your kingdom.

An Adventure in the Hall of the Hero Pathworking

This following pathworking is about elements of ourselves that are taken from us or we give away to others. These parts of ourselves are prizes, for when we access them we gain the power that was taken. This is an emotional pathworking when done correctly, and the emotion we feel is the power being restored to ourselves.

Today there will be a feast to celebrate the day when the warriors of the tribe declared you to be their chief. The fire burns brightly in the center of the hall, which is filled with the scent of burning wood. Warriors noisily shout, cheer, and dance to a song being played on a Celtic bagpipe. Wine has been flowing for some time, and everyone is a little the worse for wear.

Banging your tankard on the table, you call for silence and slowly the room comes to order.

"Warriors of the kingdom," you say in your best oration voice, "unaccustomed as I am to public speaking . . ." The room erupts into laughter but you continue. "Unaccustomed as I am to public speaking, this being the anniversary of my succession to this chair, it is time for me to declare a boon to the first warrior to touch my cup."

As you say this proclamation, you hurl your cup into the throng of drunken warriors. This is a traditional event and your warriors are ready for it. Usually the strongest and least drunk would win the resulting scramble and wrestling match. Sure enough, the warriors leap for the cup, but before they get to it, a child runs among them and grabs it.

It is a child about seven years old, with an unwashed face and wearing clothes that look like they have been stitched from some ancient material that may once have been cloth. There is stillness in the hall. None of the warriors have the heart to snatch the cup from a small child, particularly one so poor.

Suddenly one of the older warriors starts to laugh at the situation.

"It seems we have been bested by a youngster no taller than my knee; this waif must be a great warrior indeed, so the boon belongs to this child." The laughter and cheers echo around the hall as the child slowly and thoughtfully walks up to your chair.

"You seem to have lost something," the child says to you in a careful and in a measured tone.

"Yes," you say. "And what boon would you like? Clothing, a house, money?"

"If the chieftain would hear my story, maybe you would like to decide," the child says.

You agree, and the hall is hushed to hear the child's tale.

"I was born in a village close to the edge of a great forest. The people there lived in fear of the faery folk, who out of mischief would steal food and property from houses while the villagers were out in the field. Sometimes they stole children, too, and the villagers were so afraid of this that they started to leave out food for the faeries to leave their children in peace. One summer, the crops failed and there was barely enough food for the villagers, let alone leaving out any for the faery folk. So the faeries came and they took a small child, who was the offspring of a chief. They treated this child well and taught the child many things. Soon, this child started to miss human children and its parents. Initially, the faery would not let their hostage leave, but after a while, the faeries realized that the child was so unhappy they felt the young human would be happier among its own kind, and escorted the child back to the village.

"The child arrived at the location of the village, but found that time had moved on. Although only seven months had passed in the faery realm, more than seventy years had passed in the outside world, and the village was no more. The child declined the kind faeries who offered to take the child back to raise as their own, and the child decided to search for humans in other villages, because this youngster needed to be among its own kind.

"I walked until I came to this hall, and hoped that hear I might find the home I am looking for."

Blaise touches you on the shoulder. "This little child is something that has been lost to the kingdom. This waif is a part of your self that has been taken away from you, perhaps when you were very young."

You lean down to the child and ask, "What are you that has been taken away from me?"

The child tells you.

Think about what this child says. Then allocate a family for the child to live with, and know that your kingdom is stronger now that something that has been lost has been restored.

The Watchtower

Before you explore the wider aspects of your Inner Kingdom, it is important to make a reconnaissance. It is for this reason that your hall has a watchtower. If your village is attacked, the elderly and children will hide in the great hall protected by its stockade.[5] If he or she was not personally in combat, the watchtower enables the chief to see enemy troop positions and issue directions to his or her warriors on how to repel the invaders. Since Celtic fortifications were often on raised ground, a person standing in a watchtower could often see very far away and be forewarned of any impending attack.

As part of your pathworking, slowly climb the ladder in the court-yard. Below you is the village of your tribe. Immediately abutting the gate are the stables, where your mighty war chariot is stored.

The village is surrounded by a stockade and tall earth bank, but the rest of its composition is up to you. Those things that are closest to you, such as your family and friends, will have dwelling places closer to your Great Hall. A big hut could represent your workplace with lots of people going in and out. Unlike your Great Hall, the people you asso-ciate with look like they are in real life, but their role in your village might be a little different. For example, the boss in your work might be a wailing child being carried by a powerful warrior, who is in reality the boss' secretary.

From your position in the watchtower, it is possible to see how these people relate to each other. In your village, they may act differ-ently to each other from the way you would expect, because they are being seen from your unconscious perspective. In some cases, you might be unconsciously frightened of some and they may appear more fearsome in your village. The inner vision includes subtle details that you may have missed; a couple at work might have feelings for each other that you have not seen. A colleague might have been more hurt by one of your actions than you had previously thought, or someone might be secretly sharpening a dagger to stick in your back.

Be careful here, as such perceptions are often loaded by your own preconceptions. If you are worried that your partner is having an affair, and in your village you see him or her in the arms of a stranger, do not see that as evidence. All it shows is that you are convinced deeply that something is going on.

Remember, what you are seeing is a self-fulfilling prophecy unless you do something to change it, and what is manifesting in your village will actually happen to you. If you see something you do not like, it is important that you change it; however, to do that you have to step outside the walls of your Great Hall.

Looking toward the horizon, you can see other kingdoms and territory from your watchtower. These are the kingdoms of those intimately closest to you, and if you were to visit them, you would start to see them as they really are, rather than as they appear in your realm. For example, the ratcatcher in your realm may be a wonderful leader in his or her own kingdom.

Everyone rules their own Inner Kingdom and guards their borders as jealously as you. If you actually entered one of these kingdoms, you would be challenged and repelled by extremely strong forces. Sometimes a bard might appear in your hall, inviting you into another kingdom's hall, with the aim of learning something new from you. This is unlikely to be someone you know, and is more likely to be the Inner Kingdom of a spiritual guide or teacher. Some magical orders and groups have Inner Kingdoms of their own, and it is possible for them to invite you to one of these to receive instruction. It is through these inner states that people can get occult teaching without actually being a member of an esoteric order.

At the boundary of your kingdom and those of others is the forest of adventure. This is where you will spend much of your time. Once you have safely scouted from your watchtower, it is time to go out of the protection of your Great Hall and into the outside world.

The Village

You might want to explore your village in more detail first, and interact with people at a level that you would have never experienced before. Remember that what you are seeing, like anything in your Inner Kingdom, has to be interpreted symbolically rather than literally.

Firstly, check the walls of your Great Hall and stockade. Holes in the wall, or parts of the stockade that are in a poor state of repair, indicate weaknesses in your aura. It is important to find out what caused these weaknesses. Ask one of the villagers as they often know the reasons for the wall's holes or, failing that, ask Blaise. Fixing any holes will require help from a woodworker and a group of laborers. You must find these people in your village and ask them to do the work. Some of them will work for money, other times they will ask for payment in kind.

What the workers ask for payment will give you a clue as to how the problem can be fixed deep within the psyche. For example, a woman who was sexually and psychically abused by her boyfriend found herself depressed and unable to leave him. In using the village formula, she found that part of her kingdom's wall had been torn down. She asked a child how this happened and was told that she had ordered the wall to be torn down, because she wanted a giant to have easy access to the hall. If the wall was there, he would have to batter the gate down, and so she had decided that it was easier to leave a hole there. It did not take much to realize who the giant was and that her aura was leaking like a sieve because she was not resisting the giant. Obviously, there would be no point repairing the wall if the giant was going to just tear it down again. If her wall was to be repaired, she must banish the giant from her kingdom.[6]

In this situation, the woman decided to leave her abusive partner. By coincidence, he happened to be out of town two days after she made that decision. She rallied her friends and moved out of the house before he got back. She removed everything that connected her with him (including deleting him from her address book on her cellphone) with the intention of truly banishing him from her life. Once she had recovered from the removal of her ex-boyfriend, she set about going to restore the wall in her Inner Kingdom and found that the villagers, so relieved that the giant no longer bothered them, had repaired the wall for her without asking.[7]

It is important to pay attention to the walls that surround your village. These represent the ability of your lifestyle to hold its own against the problems of the outside world. These walls should be strong, but not inflexible. This is why I have chosen the symbol of a stockade rather than a stone wall. The purpose of a stockade was that it provided a good level of defense, but was flexible enough to be expanded and contracted or even moved. Your lifestyle should be able to hold its own shape, but you must never be frightened of changing it. Once again, it is important to find out what caused the holes so that they may be filled or replaced. For a long time, I had a section of wall that kept falling down because of bad soil underneath it. By examining the houses around the breach, I worked out that the wall was my current job situation, which was no longer financially or emotionally rewarding. Enemy warriors could sally forth into the breach and weaken other areas of my life. Fixing the hole (and changing my job) meant this did not happen.

> *Remember:* Whatever you change in your personal village
> will result in a change in your immediate environment.

An Adventure in the Village Pathworking

Every life has moments of conflict, either at work or at home. This pathworking is designed to uncover the root cause of any conflict and attempt to resolve it at a psychological level.

As you leave your Great Hall to confront whatever is troubling your kingdom, you will strap on the sword of your kingdom. You might want to visit the armory and chose a spear or armor. Just take a note of what has been left out for you to wear because it will flavor your journey. The treasury door might also be open, which means that you will require money for this journey.[8] Once you are dressed and armed, you leave the Hall of the Hero and step into the village.

There is a cry from the watchtower. The village is under attack! Horns of alarm sound, and warriors rush to strap on their weapons and fetch their shields from the walls of their houses. Villagers rush to hide inside their houses, and the guards slide the huge gates shut and bolt it.

You quickly run to the watchtower by the gatehouse and climb to the tower's top, which gives you a panoramic view of the village and the hill that surrounds it. Sure enough, there are several warriors at the bottom of the hill. They had hoped to sneak in, but they were seen and the alarm was raised. Now they were at the bottom of the hill, plotting their next move.

You ask the warrior on guard duty who they are. What does he say?

You then ask if he can work out what they want of your village. What does he say?

Blaise has walked to the gatehouse and is muttering magical words over the bolts of the gate. The bolts glow with power, meaning that it will take more than a physical assault to break them.

You climb down from the watchtower and ask Blaise for advice. He looks at you and says, "You have three options: you can fight the warriors, agree to a treaty, or surrender and accept their terms."

Does Blaise suggest anything else?

The Chariot

Now it is time to leave the village and enter the dark forest of adventure. In the stable is your chariot, which is drawn by two ponies: one black and the other white. You have a chariot driver who, sometimes with some difficulty, will keep these two steeds moving in the direction you want to go.

Note the state of repair of the chariot, the horses, and the driver. The car of the chariot is a symbol of your physical body; the horses are your emotions; and the charioteer is your sense of reason. If any of these are in bad shape, it is worthwhile finding out why.

The Western Mystery Tradition is legendary for its lack of emphasis on the physical body. Unlike Eastern systems, which have their martial arts or yoga to help condition and strengthen the body, the Western Mystery Traditions tends to go toward extremes, from neglecting exercise and abstaining from certain foods, to overindulging in exercise and nourishment. Either way, the poor body gets a rough time of it. It is important to get regular exercise and eat a balanced diet. This seems to create the environment for spiritual progress; in fact, my first spiritual breakthrough happened when I started going to the gym and took up karate. Others notice improvements when they give up smoking or rectify their diet.

The emotions are always a difficult thing to control, as they will pull us in directions that we do not want us to go. One good way of governing the emotions is balancing them with the intellect. This symbol of the chariot shows that without a healthy body (a sturdy chariot), the emotions and intellect are unable to go in directions they want. Without the drive of the emotions (the horses), the chariot is not going to move, and without the direction of reason (the charioteer), the chariot is going to move uncontrollably. The charioteer must understand the ponies, and know them well enough to prevent the chariot from going to places it shouldn't.

When this combined symbol of the chariot is ready, it is time to take it into the forest of adventure.

Journeying to the Forest of Adventure Pathworking

Your village is situated on a hill. This makes the village easy to defend, as an enemy cannot drive you out and gives it a clear view of the land surrounding it. A watchtower, from which guards oversee and admit those who wish to come to trade, straddles the gateway. The two gates are made from solid oak and locked by two enormous slide bolts. As these gates swing open, they reveal a causeway and a primitive road. On either side of the causeway is a deep and wide ditch that is designed to make it hard for attackers to approach your village wall.

Once your charioteer has ridden along the causeway, the road slips quickly downhill and it is a little bumpy. You have to hang on to the sides of your chariot here as the wheels bounce off the ruts made by countless carts and chariot wheels.

After a while, the road levels out, and you are on a fairly straight road through cultivated fields. Farmers till their crops and raise sheep, cattle, and pigs on this rich farmland to provide food for the village. As you ride by, the farmers wave to you, acknowledging that this part of the world is still under your direct rule.

It is a bright and sunny day. The rhythmic drumming of the ponies' hooves seems oddly energetic in comparison to the stillness of the outside world.

Soon the farmland gives way to less cultivated land. You only recently acquire this land, and although it has been explored, it has not been fully developed. In this area, you are aware that there are magical springs in whose limpid waters you can see the future or find a magical healing. There are small villages here.

This land represents skills that you are starting to learn, the new people who are coming into your life, and newfound wisdom.

As you ride along farther, you come to the periphery of an enormous and dark forest, which surrounds your kingdom. This is an ancient forest and in it are contained many wonders and dangers.

When you banish anyone from your kingdom, they usually have to pass through this forest to the outside world. Many stay here as outlaws, causing trouble for outlying farms. Occasionally, these outlaws have been known to join marauding armies in the hope that they can have some part in your downfall and resume their previous status in the village.

The forest is magical and changes all who stay too long. Slowly, they start to become less human and more like monsters and demons. Many have been here since long before you were ruler; they are great and ancient demons who are a threat to the whole of the land and not just your little kingdom.

A number of times you have thought about building a huge wall to keep the forest dwellers from your village. But Blaise has warned you against the idea, telling you stories about several kingdoms that had built huge walls to keep evil away from their kingdoms. But outside such walls, the evil grew while people inside became effete and unable to fight any more. After a while, there would be a fire, or an earthquake, which would damage the wall, and then all manner of evil would force their way into the land and find a people too weak to resist. "It is better to watch the forest dwellers," advises Blaise. "Try to understand them and help them to reintegrate into village life. Some you will have to fight and drive deeper into the forest, but always remember they will return until they are either killed or adapted into village life." Occasionally, you will send Blaise out to bring some of those banished back to see if they are ready to return to civilization; other times you will go yourself.

The forest contains many wonders. There are hermits living in caves and huts who will dispense advice and teaching. It is full of magical groves and springs, where talking trees reveal much about nature, their goddess. There are nature elementals, the gnomes, the salamanders, the undines, and sylphs, and the nature spirits like elves, and goblins, trolls, and giants. Some live on their own, others, particularly the elves, live in established communities with hierarchies much like humans.

As your kingdom grows into a place of peace, more of these magical beings will choose to allow their part of the forest to become part of your kingdom and themselves your subjects. This will bring many magical treasures from which you and your kingdom will benefit.

> *Remember:* What you experience in the forest of adventure
> will result in changes to your inner and outer world. It will
> change habits, fears, and phobias and neurotic behavior at a
> very deep level.

As you face each trial, you will face those parts of yourself that you sought to banish from your life. In reintegrating them, you become a more complete and strong person. Sometimes you will find imprisoned princesses or princes. These will be parts of yourself you gave away to other people, perhaps to a relationship or a parent in order to please them. Often, these parts are protected by the memory or fear of that person you gave a piece of yourself to, and in their Inner Kingdom these people often appear as some kind of monster. The monster's defeat will bring back what you have lost, and often provide you with a clue about fixing the problem. This is the essence behind the shamanic technique of soul retrieval, which seeks to make a person whole.

The Tiny Giant

This following passive pathworking result is of a type I called psychological magic, which will be examined in detail in the next chapter.

Here is an example of how a psychological change can be brought about in this pathworking. A very short woman believed her self-confidence had been demolished by her ex-boyfriend, who used his greater physical size to intimidate her. Having left her abusive partner, this woman now found it impossible to have another relationship, as she felt too shy to approach anyone new.

When taking part in a pathworking similar to the "Journeying to the Forest of Adventure," she saw herself locked in a tower, guarded by an enormous version of her former partner. She had been always intimidated by his larger size and sheer physical presence, and this dread meant frequently bowing to his will for fear of violence from him. But when she had stood up to him, he raped her to confirm his physical prowess. The answer was obvious: if she was bigger than him, he could not abuse her. In real life and her Inner Kingom, she was only five-foot-one, but in her Inner Kingdom where magic rendered everything possible, she set out in search of a potion to make her giant sized. In another glade she found a wizard. This wizard said that if the woman put on a magical ring she would become a giant: the only problem was that if one wore the ring, one could never take it off. The reason the wizard had never attacked the giant was because he was frightened of always being so big, but a warrior maiden like her should have no problems, if she had courage. The woman put the magic ring on and became a giantess. She faced the giant who represented her ex-partner, and he fled before her. Upon freeing the princess, she had a sudden surge of emotional power, as if something had been returned to her. She realized that since her teens she had associated her powerlessness with her height, although power is really a state of mind. Her realizing this, and suddenly having access to a part of herself that had remained locked up because of her insecurity, caused an emotional revelation about herself.

When looking at this case, it is possible to see how the woman's imagination drew her to a conclusion that was slightly different from her own idea of the problem. She had always believed that her ex-partner was responsible for creating her insecurity, rather than the relationship being a symptom of the wider problem. It is also interesting how she unconsciously generated the wizard in the imagination who had a "cure" that fixed her true problem.

Meeting Other Beings in the Forest

Earlier I said that the forest of adventure contained nonhuman beings. These are creatures like faeries, goblins, and elves. While it is possible that such forces have made an appearance in your Inner Kingdom, it is more likely that they represent magical potential within you or random parts of your self that are not under clear control or direction. Just because they might only be part of your psyche does not mean that you treat them any differently! In fact, you should treat these nonhuman elements as if they really were existing like those characters appearing in myth. This suspension of disbelief is a vital part of pathworking and in this case enables the magic that these beings represent to actually work.

If your pathworking takes you to an elven feast, you will politely ask to speak to the elven queen. In the case of Thomas the Rhymer, the elven queen liked him so much that she gave the young man the gift of poetry and song. This gift represents that magical part of the psyche unlocking its latent powers. I know one creative writer who managed to write a novel after a series of successful Inner Kingdom encounters with an elven queen. Not only did he dedicate the book to his faery queen, but also named his baby girl after her.[9]

Care needs to be exercised when dealing with the inner representations of faeries and nature spirits, as they can be quite harmful. Like their counterparts in legend, faeries and their ilk can be devious, malicious, and want to play with your mind. In some pathworkings they will represent rogue complexes or irrational parts of your character, so it is vital that you are in control when they appear. Information is your best weapon and you should read all you can about faery legends, so you know how people were tricked, and dealt the faery folk in return. There is much commonsense lore tied up in these legends and if you don't see the links when you are reading them, your unconscious mind will present the same principles in an understandable way when you do your pathworkings.

Guides and Hermits

The forest of adventure contains beings that represent your higher aspects. These appear as guides and wise ones. When they appear, it is interesting to understand what they are trying to tell you, as they can often give clues to the resolution of a particular problem or issue.

In some cases, there may be a psychic communication with another entity, either a human or what is known amongst some occult groups as an inner plane teacher. Some care needs to be taken here, as almost 95 percent of contacts made in a subjective meditation are likely to be aspects of the self. There are far too many people who claim they are in personal communication with a spiritual entity in their meditations.

Of these, few have a genuine contact, and those that do can't contact their spiritual entities in every meditation session. The reason is that to keep such threads of communication pure, a person has to disable the personality to such an extent that the message is unimpeded by the wish-fulfillment drive of the lower self. This takes an enormous effort, which, given the egos of many in the esoteric world, is a little like asking someone to stop breathing for a couple of hours.

In worst-case scenarios, they can be beings that are actually harmful to your development. If good guys exist on the astral plane, it is logical to assume that there are some inner plane beings who are not nice. As in all Inner Kingdom conversations, you have to be careful. A good rule of thumb is that no good inner plane being, or higher aspect of yourself, will ever tell you what to do. At best, they will only suggest and not really care if you ignore their advice. Like the outer plane worlds, the bad guys work by flattery, bribery, and cajolery to convince you that their way is the best. If anyone arrives and tells you that you are to head a New Age religion and that you are really the Son of God (or the Devil), it is probably a good bet that they are not a good contact, or they are a megalomaniac aspect of your own persona. The best-at-being-bad guides are those who suggest little things at first and gradually increase their demands while simultaneously inflating the ego.

You should not assume that because a being shows up dressed in the form of a god or a historical personality that they really are (or were) that being. Often, the form is simply a symbol for what that guide represents, or is created from the wish fulfillment of the meditator. A head of a magical school, to which I once belonged, had a contact with an inner plane being who had many forms, but the most common was the Egyptian god of the dead, Anubis. A disproportionate amount of her students had this god making appearances as their contact in their meditations. Being charitable, it is possible that they associated teaching with this particular human being, and wanted to be plugged into the same source. Being uncharitable, it could be a wish that they were just as important as the head of the school. This does not mean that the students were not in communication with something, or even the highest aspects of their selves, when addressing the Egyptian god of the dead. It was just that their unconscious minds had built an imaginary vehicle for teaching, and their Higher Self or the inner plane contact used it as a symbol.

Another issue is the problem of asking the guide practical information about your life and accepting this advice as gospel. No guide will ever offer you advice on such matters; they will only tell you the principles behind the problem. Guides do not tell you to dump your boyfriend or what best brand of toaster to buy, but they will tell you about the nature of relationships and how fire elementals convert bread into toast.

Guide figures can be in a pathworking to highlight deeper aspects to the issue that you are mediating upon. Hermits or guides are archetypal figures, which can, if you let them, bypass aspects of your personality that stand in the way of a clear message to the rest of yourself.

When you are building a pathworking through the forest, it is always best to allow yourself a stopover near a sacred well or a hermitage. If such a place is inhabited, then it is possible to talk to one of the sorts of characters that live there. Sometimes, they will speak in riddles or in strange, seemingly meaningless phrases. This is because, as I said in the previous chapter, the unconscious mind is blocking the message because the lower self is frightened that you will actually act upon it and the lower self will be forced to change. Like a dream, this message can be pieced together with some thought, or by example when the pathworking progresses.

In a pathworking a hermit once told me with great pomp and ceremony that wishing for "custard squares out of the refrigerator did not deliver Danish pastries; the cook has to get into the kitchen." When I asked him what he meant, the hermit just repeated what he had just said. At the time, it made no sense, but afterward I remembered that when I was a child my mother made really nice Danish pastries and custard squares with real chocolate icing. She only did made them once or twice because these sweets were too difficult to make, and despite the pleas of my sister and I, we could never get her to make more of them. Later, when I became good at cooking, I never made them, presumably because of my mother's complaint that they were too difficult to make. Custard squares and Danish pastries had become a symbol for something nice that I had waited for in vain. What the hermit was trying to tell me was that in such matters the only alternative is for me to create my own. Oddly, the issue I was mediating upon was nothing to do with my parents, or cooking in general, it was about latent skills that I had never developed. My lower self, therefore, had a vested interest in keeping this information secret, because I would then spend a lot of time doing more creative work and less time in front of the television.

Sometimes a hermit or similar being will offer to guide you through a particular scenario. When this happens, you should be careful not to simply blindly follow the guide but remain aware of what is happening. I can remember one scenario where my guide took me through all sorts of adventures and walking around in circles. When I berated him for it, he laughed and asked if I had "got the message yet." In my case, the question I was pondering was about my dependence on a particular spiritual teacher. What my Higher Self was trying to tell me was that I should never be entirely reliant on another being for wisdom.

In the Inner Kingdom pathworking I have designed for this book, the character of Blaise is a guide and a source of wisdom. If you design your own symbolic Inner Kingdom, you might like to replace him with a similar archetypal figure, like Merlin, Thomas Aquinas, Plato, or John Dee. There is no need to have a historical character either; figures like *Star War*'s Obi Won Kenobi or Yoda work well if you are moved by that symbolism. *Star Trek* is full of similar archetypes to draw upon, as does Tolkien's *Lord of the Rings* or, if you have a really good sense of humor, the Harry Potter series of children's books.

Meeting the Wise Woman Pathworking

The following pathworking is designed to give you a link to the feminine energy of the Earth. This particular pathworking provides advice, but not in an intellectual way. When people have tried this particular pathworking, they have found that the wise woman does not say anything, but instead they receive a feeling of warmth and of love. Others have found this exercise hard because it deals with the Mother archetype and they have had difficulty with their own mothers. Some of the symbolism of this pathworking is associated with the Mother and Venus archetypes, however, the majority is taken from an Arthurian legend of Owain, with a slightly different end result. The "Meeting the Wise Woman" pathworking will give you an answer to some of the questions you might have relating to life and death, and also has a strong redemptive element, making the pathworking very effective at removing pain and hurt. Its use was taught to me by a very clever priestess who loved to stir things up in my life for a while—which is exactly what this pathworking does.

The road opens out into a clearing, and there is a narrow track off to the left. A glint of copper in the trees catches your eye, and you leave your chariot to investigate.

Walking down the narrow path, you notice that everything has gone quiet. You enter a clearing, which is covered with wild wheat. In the center are a well, a fir tree, and an ancient stone. Hanging from a tree branch by three lead chains is a copper bowl. It is such a strange combination of things; you are left wondering what to do. Suddenly, your thoughts are interrupted by the appearance of a tiny, dark man emerging from behind the well.

"Hello," he says. "I would not even think about doing that if I were you."

"Doing what?" you ask, confused.

"Lots of people have done it, but she has always got them."

"Who? Do what?" You are starting to get a little cross that the man is not actually telling you much.

"The wise woman. She is summoned by pouring water on the rock. But the danger is that when she comes, nothing is ever the same again."

"What does she do?" you ask.

"Some she kills, others she rewards, but no one comes away un-scarred." He pauses. "You are going to do it, aren't you?"

"I thought I might."

"Hell's bells, another sucker!" says the man. "Don't say you were not warned!" And with that he turns on his heels and runs into the forest.

You take the copper dish from the chain and fill it with water from the well. You notice that there is the sound of humming all around you, and a gentle breeze whistles through the fir tree. The sun goes behind a cloud.

Here it goes, you mentally say, and pour water on the rock.

Suddenly, there is a clap of thunder. Dark storm clouds fill the sky and the wind becomes stronger.

The earth starts to shake and you lose your balance.

Rain pours down from the sky, and the wind becomes so strong that it is impossible to stand even if the earth were not shaking.

Then, as suddenly as it all began, it stops. First the shaking stops, then clouds part, and finally the sun shines again. There is a fluttering of wings, and hundreds of birds fly into the tree and start to sing. It is all so beautiful, and you feel relaxed. *Surely nothing can be so bad now,* you think. Then you notice the dark shape enter the glade.

He is a warrior, dressed from head to toe in black. On his head, covering his face, is a dark helmet. He has a huge slashing sword of coal-colored iron in his left hand.

"Who is it that poured water on the wise woman's stone?" the warrior says.

"I did, but I meant no harm," you said.

"Harm or no, the punishment for pouring the sacred water on the stone is death," he says as he advances toward you.

"Can't we talk about this?" you ask, drawing your sword.

"No, the universe is a fairly difficult place to understand at times, and dealing death gives me a sense of purpose," says the warrior, swinging his sword at you.

"Well, everyone has to have a purpose in life," you say, parrying his blows.

"Glad you see it that way," the black warrior says.

"Not at all," you reply.

The fight becomes a complex ballet of swordplay. Sparks fly as you each fight your way across the glade. You seem easily matched, and each slash he makes you can parry and vice versa.

After some time, the action gets tiring, and the black warrior lets down his guard for a moment, allowing you a clear overhand blow to his helmet.

The helmet splits.

"Bugger," says the dark warrior and promptly vanishes.

Well, that was strange, you think.

Another being enters the glade. She is covered from head to toe in a black cloak.

"Er, hello," you say, fully aware that the last person wearing black advancing upon you attempted to kill you.

"Hail to thee, slayer of the black warrior. Why do you approach the wise woman of the forest?"

You think about this. *Why would anyone embark on a quest for knowledge?* "I seek to know in order to serve," you reply.

"Serve who?"

"The land and its people, for I am their chief."

The woman draws back her hood, and looks straight at you into the depths of your soul.

"I am she whom you seek to serve, and you are born of my blood," she says.

"What would you ask of me?"

You ask her any question, and she will reply. After she has finished, she says, "I am the river in which you sink and are supported. I am the water that carries you through life toward the endless sea, where all life becomes one. I am with you until the sun has left the sky, until I wash at the waters for you at the ford on the morning of your last fatal battle, and carry your soul to the Isle of Apples. Unlock your clasping hands on your cares. All the pain that I mixed into your life enables joy to be born. Holding the pain as a fist cages joy's flight. Come to me, and let me wash the pain away."

And with that, she takes water from the well and pours it over your head. The water does not feel like water, and it feels like the liquid is healing you. Any pain you have felt starts to subside and any tension you may have is released.

She says, "You may return to my glade whenever you need such healing."

And with that, she vanishes.

Notes

When this inner world map of the Hall of the Hero was tested upon several groups of people, there were some interesting results that fall into the category of psychological magic (of which we will look at in the next chapter). The first result was that although the design of the hall was the only thing that was really described, there was an unconscious urge on many of the participants to change the layout. (Those that know something of Cabbalah will be aware that I have based it on the Tree of Life model.) More than one person wanted to change the rooms around. One in particular thought it was important that the room dedicated to her partner should be placed behind her, instead of where the room dedicated to the Father God (which has a connection to the archetype of the Father), and her parents should really be in those front rooms, where she could see them. Psychologically, what she was saying was that she felt the need to "replace" her father with her partner, and place the role models of her parents in full view instead of in the shadows behind her.

Another found her warriors made too much noise and she could not feel comfortable. She also did not feel like she had any control over them, and became a little frightened and frustrated. When asked if she had a busy life, she replied that her life was too busy, with too many things going on for her to cope with, and she felt out of control. Another woman, who had just left her depressing husband after many years of being focused on him, found that there were few warriors in the hall. This was because all the parts of her had been focused on a man who was no longer there; effectively, he had all her warriors! Her first response was to use the remaining warriors to recruit some more from the village and outlying region.

These examples are indications that the Inner Kingdom was working. All of these things show that the unconscious was using the pathworking to tell the participants something about themselves. Everything that happens, every desire you feel in your Inner Kingdom, is a symbolic clue to your true state of being.

The pathworking had also given the opportunity for the pathworkers to actually change those things about themselves they didn't like. The woman who felt that she was not in control of her Inner Kingdom could visualize herself banging her sword on the table and ordering her unruly warriors to be quiet. It is easier to gain control of the beings of your Inner Kingdom than it is those in the material world. But once control has been obtained, and you acknowledge yourself as the ruler of your Inner Kingdom, this action will start to percolate down the planes until you equally are in control of your material world. The warrior-deficient woman found that after she had issued her order to find more troops, she found herself surrounded by new friends.

CHAPTER FOUR

Using Imagination to Change Your Psyche

The previous chapters of this book have shown how pathworking can have psychological effects. The aim of this chapter is to focus specifically on this mental facility and use it to find weaknesses in the psyche and repair them. The techniques we will look at are the result of some seven years of experimentation with a variety of different people. During that time, we found a fairly simple formula that could be examined as part of an ongoing therapy. Although occultists, not psychologists, developed this pathworking, some of the counselors in England who were asked to comment on this pathworking's effectiveness tried it out with some spectacular successes.

Psychological magic is based on the occult concept of working on the astral level with the images that rise in a person's mind during a passive pathworking.[1] As I have said, earlier occultists knew that these images, which are generated mostly by the lower self or lower personality, had a direct effect on the World of Material in which a person lived, and changing those images enabled a person to change his or her material world. But in the early 1990s, a few of us started to reason that if these images were being changed, there must also be a fundamental change in the person's psyche to bring them about. People who mentally think of themselves as "losers" can never achieve success in occult terms unless they lose the elements in their psyche that make them destroy their own life. So it is reasonable to assume that if the power of pathworking was brought to bear on the psyche, it would be possible to find out the root causes of neuroses and eliminate them at the source.

The effect was explosive, particularly as the early experiments started to coincide with dramatic changes in all our lives. I personally think this was because those neurotic crutches that had propped us up all our lives where suddenly kicked out from underneath us. Married couples suddenly discovered that the reasons they were together were not actually based on love, but a desire to mimic the disasters of their parents. Another subject found that his hatred of women was based, not on competition with his brother as he always thought, but on a long-forgotten incident of adolescent sexual abuse; a pagan found that his early Christian upbringing was still having a dramatic effect on the sort of relationships he was choosing. While this self-discovery was one thing, the magical altered state of the passive pathworking gave the people a chance to change their psychological response to the various parts of their past and build a new future.

Unfortunately, this technique did stir things up too much. It seems that if one removed a single neurosis, like a house of cards much of that person's worldview came crashing down with it. While many would consider such techniques dangerous, the occultist, along with the alchemist, accepts this particular stage as vital to becoming a true "integrated" person, i.e., someone whose personality works in tune with his or her Higher Self. The result of this pathworking technique is an initial feeling of empowerment, as energy trapped in the neurotic complex is freed. This is followed by a sense of purpose for the future, and then sometimes by an urge to return to the safety of the past. Some reported a sense of depression, as the roadmap for their life felt altered, and the things that previously gave them joy were suddenly tasteless shadows. In alchemy this period is called *nigredo*, which, according to the great sixteenth-century alchemical text "The Rosary of the Philosophers," is when the brain turns black.[2] Alchemy describes in horrific terms what this stage feels like using the imagery of rotting corpses. From this mass of depression rise the buds of something greater, which the alchemists called *albedo* (whitening), wherein this blackness is purified.

Fortunately, this type of nigredo period following the pathworking session was rarely as bad as was described by alchemists, because the technique was only focused on one aspect of the psyche rather than the complete personality. Removing a selected neurosis did not usually take down a person's entire worldview all at once. However, the follow-through process was usually unpleasant. From a psychological point of view, you are rushing the person through to a realization; a process that usually takes a long time in therapy, where the conscious mind is in control and the therapist has to rely on Freudian slips, dream interpretation, and other insights to reveal the state of the unconscious mind. However, by using this pathworking technique, the unconscious mind is opened, and it is up to both patient and guide to interpret the findings.

As we have seen earlier, each personality is built from the lessons we have learned from the past. These lessons always start from a single lesson that was taught to us by experience or from teachers, friends, parents, or situations. There is an occult belief that states the first thing you hear about a subject of which you know nothing about, that information will become part of your Inner Kingdom and the basis from which you will judge all other incoming information. But that association becomes much more than that: we actually build a life based around this lesson, until the simple lesson is a complex tree of ideas linked by association. To show my point, ponder my next fairly simple example.

When I was a child of eleven years old, a role model of mine, a Christian teacher, told me that they had found chariot wheels in the Red Sea, proving that Moses had crossed the waters, holding back the sea until he closed it on pharaoh's chariots. It was an important point for me, because this little bit of knowledge covered all number of flaws I had about fundamental Christian philosophy. I reasoned that if the pharaoh's chariots had been found, then Moses had a fixed place in history and therefore was an obvious element of literal truth in Bible stories. Throughout my teens I carried this "literal" image of biblical history and its obvious association with the literal theology of fundamental Christianity. All was well until my interest in ancient history turned toward archaeology in the biblical period, and I discovered that the chariot wheel statement was complete fiction. My universe was shattered. Everything that I had been told by this teacher was now in doubt. I applied research to everything that I had accepted as fact and found it wanting, and finally I abandoned fundamentalist Christianity entirely in favor of a personal revelation. Some years later, I found a friend from that period of my life to whom fundamental Christianity remained important. He asked me why I had "abandoned my faith," and I told him about the teacher and the chariot wheels. He looked at me as if I was stupid. "But they did find chariot wheels in the Red Sea," he said. Initially, he thought he had read the information somewhere, but, like me, he was able to trace the information back to the same teaching session. Unlike me, the information that chariot wheels were not found in the Red Sea did not break his faith.

We can draw the associations that my mind made from that one incident into a tree.

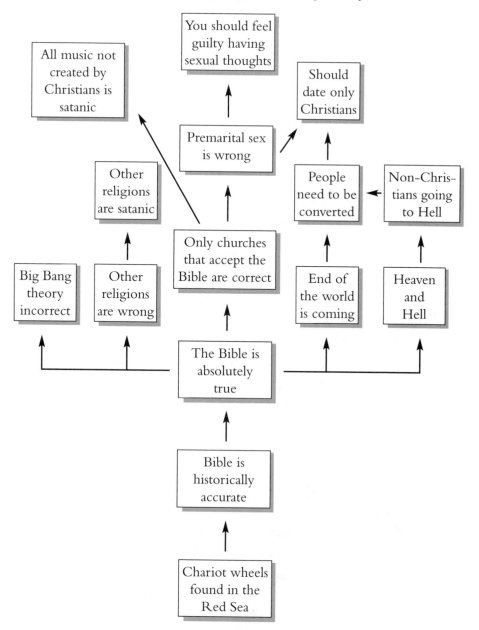

Figure 7: Association Tree Based on Incorrect Initial Information

While it would probably be shallow to suggest that my Christian faith was entirely based on that one incident, it propped up many of the fundamentalist Christian ethics that I stood by in my teenage years. Destroy the roots, which are that first association, and the entire association tree will fall. What I am describing is a loss of interest in a religion, and many who have lost their faith report something similar. An event happens that undermines the first association they had with that faith. War, for example, can shatter a person's belief if that faith was based on an association of a divine being being all-knowing and all-loving. If, one would say, if deity was all-knowing and all-loving, why was war allowed to happen?

However, this same thing applies to any belief pattern or worldview. Such a pattern begins with a single seed that grows by association after association, until it is a dominant life force. This can be good if it is a positive seed from which a life grows. My parents built much of my life around a seed form, which was "Always ask questions."[3] One school of magic, of which I was a member, described initiation as planting the seed of light. In other words, the symbolism of divinity once planted in the unconscious would build a new personality based on a divine plan. More often, the things we need to remove are the negative associations, which we may have made by accident. Remove the negative seed, and it is possible to destroy most of the associations that sprang from it. This allows new and correct information to replace the corrupted programming.

It is for this reason that the following technique uses the symbol of a tree as an accurate depiction of the problem. It cannot be a very nice tree, because this tree is in the position of causing trouble in your life now. In the technique, this tree is shown as sucking the joy from your life. Below is an outline of the formula so that is possible to discuss how it all works. We will look at the full pathworking later in this chapter, but before we give an explanation, it is important to give an outline of the process.

Outline

1. The pathworker is taken in a pathworking to a beautiful garden.

2. The pathworker is told this garden is a garden of his or her Inner Kingdom. There are pagodas representing each area of his or her life: work, family, etc.

3. The pathworker's eye is drawn to an ugly old tree, which seems out of place in the garden. Its twisted roots seem to be sucking the life out of the garden and the pagodas.

4. The pathworker approaches the tree and tries to destroy it, but discovers he or she can not.

5. A guide approaches and shows the pathworker how to get inside the tree.

6. The pathworker finds himself or herself inside the tree, and is then taken down a corridor where rooms open up into the various times when whatever is behind the complex are manifested.

7. On each occasion, the pathworker is made to confront what behavior he or she sees and change it to a more appropriate situation with a positive conclusion.

8. After at least four of these experiences (more if the guide cannot work out what the common thread is), the pathworker is guided to the roots of the tree.

9. At the roots of the tree, there is a dark room where symbols are spontaneously allowed to be generated, which illustrate the root of the problem.

10. The root of the problem is resolved using symbols and, as the tree breaks up, the pathworker plants a seed of a new affirmation. This seed grows into a white rose.

11. The pathworker sits in the petals of the rose and rises through the decaying tree to the garden.

12. The white rose has replaced the old tree, and the Inner Kingdom garden is healed.

Before the pathworking begins, the pathworker is encouraged to relax
as much as possible, but is told that he or she will always be able to describe what is seen and felt, and that the pathworker will also never
lose the ability to hear the pathworking leader's voice. (I tend to place
the pathworker in a chair in the center of the room, and walk around
the person clockwise during the pathworking. This seems to help the
process by providing energy to the person and also that the pathworker
does not associate my voice as coming from a particular direction. Direction must be defined by what the pathworker sees in the pathworking, and not by any "compass" on the earth level.)

The pathworker is taken to a beautiful, ordered garden and told
that this garden represents his or her life. The garden is a variant on an
Inner Kingdom that we looked at in the last chapter, as the different
aspects of the pathworker's life, such as work, family, etc., are seen as
things that would appear in such an ornamental garden: pagodas, pools,
bridges, trees, bandstands, summer houses, etc. These symbols are shown
in a positive aspect, to remind the pathworker that except for this problem, his or her life would be great. Although a pathworker might have
many complexes that are causing problems for the garden, it is important to tackle the problems one at a time.

The troubling complex is depicted as an ugly, out-of-place tree that
drains life from the garden. Cutting down the tree is impossible. It is
either too big, or if cut down, the tree will spring up again. Destroying
this tree is also impossible, as the roots are deep in the ground, and the
tree will rise again from the hidden roots. The pathworker must be
shown that the tree's removal is not an option, that the pathworker
must recognize and face this complex, as physically harming the tree
only represses the dysfunctional complex.

A guide is then called or comes into view to assist the pathworker
in removing the tree. Who the guide will be should be discussed before

the pathworking begins. This guide can be anything in authority that the pathworker accepts and trusts. Some people use a god or goddess as the guide; others use relatives whose wisdom or protective influence they respect. The function of this helpful guide is to make the pathworker feel comfortable and protected as he or she deals with the sometimes frightening experiences within the tree.

The guide opens the tree, and the tree becomes bigger on the inside than it is on the outside. Holding a lantern, the guide leads the pathworker deep into the complex, which is seen as a corridor carved out of the wood; the very knots in the wall whisper the voices in the subconscious that mock the pathworker with its corrosive messages.

This step of the pathworking recognizes that what a person believes is his or her own problem is more than likely just to be the tip of the iceberg. By the time a complex becomes intrusive or compulsive, it is likely to have manifested in countless other situations and experiences. Even though the pathworker is unlikely to know the root cause of the problem in the initial stages of this pathworking, it is important to see some of the complex's outcomes, and, if possible, repair some of these outcomes.

This goal is achieved by having the pathworker approach a door within a corridor within the complex. The pathworker is told that when the door opens, he or she will see the last time when the problem manifested itself. Initially, the pathworker is allowed to see the scene as is if it were a movie. Then the leader asks how the pathworker feels about what happened. The pathworker is then asked to experience the scene, but as if he or she was there in the first place. Again, the pathworker is asked how he or she feels and if he or she could have done anything better. Then the pathworker is given the opportunity to change the scene where he or she acts in a stronger, more confident way. It does not matter if the change is absurd; it is just important that the outcome is altered to become more positive.

For example, one woman had trouble with her boss of whom she was terrified. The first door opened, and a scene replayed where he was bullying her. When the scene played out, she could see that herself as frightened and, more to the point, her boss could see that fear. She could also see that her boss was enjoying the fear he instilled in her. When she sat in as herself in the scene, she could see the fear, too, but as she examined her feelings she was having at that moment, she was also feeling deep anger. She realized that the fear was actually of what would happen if she got angry. When asked what the best way she could allow that anger to be expressed to her boss would be, the woman decided she should tell her boss he was wrong. She visualized herself stripping down her boss' arguments before giving him a piece of her mind on his deficiencies as a manager and a human being. She saw her bully fold and start to cry. Later, she would find that the seed cause of this incident was something her father used to do. Her father had not particularly liked or wanted children, and made it clear to his children that they were not allowed to be noisy. He actually hit them until they realized that loud noises were a bad idea. When she was four, she fell down the stairs and broke her arm, and howled in pain. The father, not realizing her injury, shouted at her for being noisy, cuffed her, and returned to the living room. The child's mother intervened, but the father, ashamed, didn't apologize, and pretended that the incident did not happen. The child had received the impression that it was important never to express anything, even under extreme conditions, and it was acceptable for men to bully her.

In psychological magic, the seed of any problem is revealed deep in the tree's roots. After tracking the various branches, the pathworker is lead into a hole in the corridor and told that this hole leads to roots of the complex. The pathworker goes into the hole and slides down the inside of the roots. Deep into the earth the pathworker slides, until he or she emerges in a dark cave. The pathworker is reassured that his or her guide is present too.

After a while, the pathworker is told that symbols will come into his or her mind, which must be interpreted quickly by the leader. This interpretation takes some skill, particularly as the leader has to intuit what the symbol may mean for that particular pathworker, but this task of interpretation can be made easier by the earlier journeys into the person's past. The pathworker undergoing the technique will have to say everything he or she sees, no matter how apparently silly or absurd it may sound.

The guide is then required to find a solution to the problem using the symbols that have been generated by the unconscious mind of the pathworker performing the technique.

One of the more spectacular examples of this complex-solving pathworkings came with one overachieving woman, Liz, who was depressed and burned-out. Throughout the initial parts of the psychological magic pathworking, she had found out her problems was connected to a work ethic that came from her parents. Throughout her successful university career, she regretted not getting drunk or having a sexual partner because she was working too hard. One of her earliest memories was of being chided for playing in mud when she should have been cleaning her room.

When led to the dark room, Liz initially saw a little girl dressed in red, which was the "naughty" side of herself, which she allowed to merge into her. Initially, the guide thought that was the end of it, however, this dialogue occurred between Liz and her guide:

Liz: "I see a little, blonde-haired girl in a dress skipping toward me. She seems perfect . . . as she gets closer I am feeling colder . . . I don't like this."

Guide: "It is okay . . . who do you think the little girl is?"

Liz: "It is me . . . when I said she was perfect, she is all that I was expected to be. She is so cold, and I am getting more and more drained the closer she gets."

Guide: "That is because maintaining that image is taking so much of you. That little girl has many of the qualities that you need. She enabled you to work hard and achieve; you don't want to abandon her. Lean into her heart and take what you want from her. . . . See it as a ball of light. Place it in your own heart."

Liz: "She has turned into a little plastic doll's face. Like there is no life left in her. She has crumbled and vanished."

This particular image moved Liz very much and afterward changed her view of life dramatically. No longer did she need to be the good little girl; she could do and be who she wanted to be. In fact, she left her husband, whom she married because he had asked her and she didn't want to offend him by saying no. Liz changed her stressful job, which she hadn't wanted to leave because everyone depended on her, and found a new life free from her parents' role model for her.

Here is another example, this time from Colin, who was having sexual relationship difficulties:

Colin: "The room is lighting up. I see a coffin."

Guide: "Go over and look at it."

Colin: "There is a dead person it. He looks like a bishop; he has a crook in the coffin with him and is wearing a miter. He is perfectly preserved; he looks like he is just asleep."

Guide: "What does that mean to you?"

Colin: "He is a religious authority. But when I was religious, I didn't like this sort of religion. I was a happy clappy—this is more Catholic stuff."

Guide: "What do you know about Catholic priests?"

Colin: "Dunno, they are celibate. . . . Oh, that is it. This sex stuff is linked to religion. I thought it was better to remain celibate outside marriage. But I don't understand, I stopped being a

Christian a long time ago and have had lots of relationships since."

Guide: "But a dead bishop has been carried around in your unconscious since."

Colin: "Maybe."

Guide: "What does this scene remind you of?"

Colin: "It looks like those pictures of pilgrims visiting a saint or holy relic . . . holy relic of the past, I guess."

Guide: "A revered holy relic."

Colin: ". . . that I superstitiously hang on to?"

Guide: "Despite your religious beliefs moving on."[3]

Colin: "Okay. I respect those beliefs in others but I don't want to worship them any more. We need a Reformation here."

Guide: "Okay. I want you to imagine that Martin Luther is with you."

Colin: "Okay." (laughs)

Guide: "How does he think this reformation should go?"

Colin: "He is saying I must be the bishop and wake up."[5]

Guide: "Okay. I want you to hold Luther's hand and allow yourself to merge with the bishop."

Colin: "Lie on a corpse, yuck!"

Guide: "It is worse than that; you are going to merge yourself with the corpse. Lie on top and allow yourself to sink into it."

Colin: (after a while) "Okay, I feel very cold, clinical, and like part of me is not working. It is like I could soar spiritually, but at the same time I am missing the point of the earth. I feel set in this stone coffin . . . like I can't get out."

Guide: "Are you still holding Luther's hand?"

Colin: "Yes, he has his eyes shut."

Guide: "He is praying for a reformation."

Colin: "I feel weird . . . there is energy coming into me."

Guide: "When you feel you can, I want you to sit up."

Colin: "This is hard . . . done it. Hang on, the body is still there."

Guide: "Are you still wearing the clothes?"

Colin: "Yes, but so is the corpse."

Guide: "That is okay. Get out of the coffin. (pause) Take off the miter and the robes, and place them in the coffin. Imagine that you are dressing in the clothes you are a wearing today. What is Luther doing?"

Colin: "He is still praying."

Guide: "The bishop's body is crumbling into dust . . . like you see in those old vampire movies. The robes and the bishop's crook are burning."

Colin: "Yes. There is nothing left."

Guide: "A group of people has arrived. They are wearing modern clothes and look like modern worshippers. They slide the coffin lid shut. One of them tells you that 'the past is gone, we do things differently now.'"

The scene fades and Colin is left in darkness with Martin Luther.

The End of the Complex

To maximize the effect of the magical imagination pathworking, the pathworker has to see the destruction of the complex and the flowering of something new developing from it. This is powerfully illustrated by the planting of a new spiritual seed in the darkness while the tree splits apart at a molecular level. The new seed, based on a new affirmation, grows into a white rose, which is a symbol of a pure desire, and replaces the tree as it collapses into dust.

In the above example, there was an earthquake as the tree started to break up. Martin Luther handed Colin a seed. Colin visualized what he wanted as a scene taking place within the seed. He planted the seed, which quickly grew into a huge, white rose, filling the room with a beautiful scent. Colin sat in the center of the rose, which continued to grow upward through the carnage of the exploding tree, finally emerging into the bright sunlight. As he looked down, Colin saw there was not a trace of the tree left.

A Guide to the Risks

Although I would like to say this system is completely safe and easy, it isn't. This pathworking places a great deal of strain on the leader and the pathworker. People with the skills of being leaders in psychological magic are either experienced counselors or have got the knack of empathizing with people's psyches. If you haven't these skills, it is better that you don't try it.

Pathworking leaders have be intuitive enough to see the direction that the pathworking is heading, while at the same time being ready for the pathworking to head somewhere not anticipated. Leaders are in a position of complete trust, and information disclosed must never be talked about outside of the session, although anonymous case studies are allowed. The leaders have to be extremely well versed in symbolism, and preferably be a trained counselor or psychologist. Also, people who are skilled at interpreting dreams will probably also be good leaders.

The leaders also should know when they have to back off and leave the healing of the complex to professionals. An example of this was when I encountered a pathworker who suddenly, much to their surprise and mine, started to reveal that he had been sexually abused. Initially, this pathworker was unhappy to reveal this memory but, thinking it was something else, I pressed ahead. There is a certain amount of foresight involved in being a guide, and suddenly I saw the head of something dark start to emerge in the pathworking. This head, which had been so well buried in this person's unconscious, made me realize that this pathworker would require more expertise. That particular session was bought to a halt, and the pathworker was recommended to see a traditional mental health counselor.

Another risk is that leaders might unconsciously impose their perceptions onto the pathworkers and guide them to a conclusion. Unlike traditional counseling, leaders can suggest reasons why a problem may manifest, but the pathworker is always correct and the leader must not impose his or her moral, religious, or political views upon the pathworkers. If a pathworker is covering up the desire to have multiple sex partners, it is not up to the leader to decide that the pathworker's desire is morally wrong and regard it as "part of the neurosis." However, if the pathworker has repressed a strong sex drive, it is valid that pathworking be used to find why that expression has been suppressed. As they are in a position of power, leaders need to know themselves well enough to put aside their own personal beliefs when taking part in the technique.

The hardest position for a group leader involved in such a pathworking is what happens if the pathworker divulges a complex that has resulted in a crime. I am lucky in that I have not encountered this situation yet, but my view would be that if this disclosure is bothersome to the leader, he or she should close down the working and suggest that the pathworker seek more professional help. A councilor or psychotherapist will know exactly what to do.

Neither should leaders try psychological magic on a psychiatrically ill person, unless the leader is medically qualified to do so. Although I know psychologists and counselors who use this technique, this book is written mostly for laypeople who want to help friends who are finding their lives difficult because of some neurosis. Psychological magic pathworking is best at tackling the causes of mild depression with the depression's roots in some intangible past, neurotic behavior, and minor obsessive and compulsive behavior.

If you are ever in doubt when performing, taking part, or completing the psychological magic pathworking technique, don't do it! If ever in doubt during a pathworking, allow the pathworker to return to the garden and end it.

A person should not undergo more than one pathworking in a month—preferably there should be a three-month gap between exposures to the technique. This is because the pathworker needs to adapt to the fallout from the collapse of the complex, which confuses the psyche. There is also a considerable amount of stirring of the unconscious, which can make the person appear worse in the short term, as the mind processes the experience to build a new worldview.

Below is the script for the technique to be read to a pathworker. Obviously, there are gaps in the process for the pathworker to describe what he or she sees and feels. The pathworking is to be read in a slow, even voice. The script is also devoid of much descriptive language, although it is packed with words to encourage descriptive thought.

The Technique

Just relax, and regulate your breathing, slowly and deeply. As you breathe out, you will breathe out stress, and as you breathe in, you will relax more.

(Pause)

Now throughout this you will always hear the sound of my voice, and you will always be able to speak to me. Is that okay?

Just relax. You are in a beautiful garden. You feel warm and comfortable; it is a bright summer's day. All around you are flowers and trees; the garden is well ordered. This is your garden, it represents your life. All around you are pagodas, pools, and summerhouses, which represent the different parts of your life. There is one for your work, another for your home.

All is content and pleasant. It is a warm, clear day, and you feel that you might just want to relax and fall asleep in your garden.

Then you see a tree that you have not noticed before.

The sun goes behind a cloud.

While everything in your garden looks beautiful, this tree is out of place. It is dark and twisted. It seems to suck light out of the air, and its roots have erupted out of the ground. This tree is sucking the life out of plants around it, and as you look, you can see the roots are spreading and where they travel the surrounding plants look sick. The roots head toward some of the pagodas and are undermining their foundations.

This tree is no good, you say, it has to go.

You go up to the tree. How can you get rid of it? If you cut it down, with its extensive root network, it will simply grow again. You need help with this problem.

A voice says, "You need to destroy this tree from within." You see (insert name of guide). In the guide's hand is a staff. The guide says, "However, the journey will be hard, and you will have to face many difficulties. Are you ready to do that?"

You nod, and the guide lights a lamp for you and strikes the tree with the staff. The bark of the tree parts like a curtain to reveal that the trunk is hollow. The guide tells you that you only have to think the word RETURN to come back to the garden and then the technique will be safely over. You nod, the guide enters the tree, and you follow.

You are in a hollow tunnel shaped out of living wood. The walls are heavily knotted, and you can here a subtle whispering.

(Whisper) "Failure, loss, depression, and despair." [5]

The guide tells you that, to understand what caused the tree to grow, you first must examine its branches. The guide takes you to a long corridor lined with doors and says, "Behind each of these doors are moments when the problem first manifested. When you look behind these doors, you will see a scene that will show the problem and contributed to building this tree. Then we will get a chance to change that scene so that it never happened. This will weaken the tree and make it easier to kill." The guide takes you to a door, and tells you that this is the last time that the problem manifested in your life. You open the door and shine your light into the room. What do you see? (The pathworker will describe the scene.)

How do you feel? (The pathworker will describe how he or she feels.)

Now I want you to take the part of yourself in this. Just allow yourself to become part of the scene and allow it to replay. How do you feel now? (The person will describe how he or she feels.)

Do you think that there is a better way to handle this? (The pathworker says yes or no, and describes a method he or she thinks will work. Assist him or her to reach a conclusion however absurd it might appear.)

Now I want you to play out that same scene doing what we have just worked out. What happens? (The pathworker will describe what happens.)

That event now has happened like that, okay? The harm that it caused is now undone. Step out of that room.[6] Now I want you to go to pick a door from midway down the corridor. Your guide tells you that this one will lead you to a point where the problem manifested several years ago.

You open the door and go through the same sequence as before. When that scene is complete, repeat it about four or five times. Each time should lead you closer to the original incident that caused the problem. (*Note:* The last time will be the situation that caused the problem, although it is important that you do not tell the person that.)

Right! Your guide believes you are finally ready to approach the seed of the tree, now you have a rough idea of how it has affected you. Are you ready?

(Wait until the pathworker says yes.)

Your guide leads you to a hole in the wall. This is a hollow root that leads directly to the source of the problem. Slide down the root and you will find yourself in a cave. There you will receive symbolic impressions. It does not matter how silly they appear; I want you to tell me what you see, okay?

(Wait until the pathworker says yes.)

You jump into the hole, which turns out to be a long slide deep, deep into the earth. You emerge in a dark cave. You are aware that the guide is behind you, so you are safe. After a while, you will start to see images. What are they? (The pathworker will describe what he or she sees. You will have to think quickly to work out what the symbols mean. Then you will have work out a fairly dramatic way of using those symbols to resolve the pathworker's problem [see examples later]. When that is done . . .)

The ground is beginning to shake; the tree is beginning to crumble from within. We do not have much time. Your guide hands you a seed. It is about the size of a large marble and is pearl colored. Now I want you to visualize a scene that would show you being what you want to be, without this problem. I want you to see it as clearly as possible, living within the seed. Okay?

(Wait until the pathworker says okay. It might be helpful if you have agreed on this image beforehand.)

Plant the seed. Your guide hands you a watering can, and you water the seed. Almost at once, the seed shoots up and quickly grows into a bush with an enormous white rose bud. The bud opens, and the room is full of its scent. This causes the old tree to start to dissolve quicker. You sit in the rose petals, which feels like a soft bed. The rose grows upward, taking you with it.

The tree is dissolving.

The knots that locked up feelings of negativity are unlocking, freeing up the trapped energy they contained. Earth from the garden is rushing to fill in the void left by the dead tree.

Suddenly, you burst into the sunlight of the garden. Blinking from the brightness, you see the last parts of the tree dissolving into dust. You step out of the rose and watch it grow into an enormous tree with many beautiful roses. Already the plants that surround the site of the old tree are healing. You look to see where its roots had undermined the pagodas and summerhouses and instead see small white flowers.

It is as if the tree was never there.

The garden is healed.

Lie down in the garden, knowing at that all is well. Relax for now. When you open your eyes, you will be aware of this time and space. You will remember everything. Slowly, and in your own time, open your eyes.

Afterward

It is very important that you talk the whole event through with the pathworker afterward so that some of the details can be made clear to him or her. The pathworker will also feel a bit disorientated, so he or she should also have something to eat or drink to help ground the scattered energies.

Psychological Magic Pathworkings

Besides the psychological magic technique, there are pathworkings designed to help people out of specific situations. I have included two here as examples because they will enable you to think about how to approach writing some of your own pathworkings. Unlike the above method, these pathworkings are not interactive. The pathworker is simply led through them. All of these pathworkings assume that you have relaxed the pathworker completely beforehand and have allowed him or her to visualize a doorway.

Healing the Parental Archetypes

This pathworking is designed for those who have parental images that are so corrupted that the existence of their mother or father is a complete blight on their lives. An example would be the daughter of a prostitute whom I mentioned earlier. It is also for those who, for various reasons, lack a father or mother figure in their life. Often children can bond with foster parents, but in some cases this is not possible, and these children lack a good Father or Mother archetype to base their life upon. This can lead to confusion in relationships as they get older, or a tendency to find people who approximate to the nearest role model but may not be appropriate.

This pathworking forms a link with the Husband and Wife archetypes of Isis and Osiris, whose love was so great they could conceive their child Horus even after death. Isis makes an ideal mother image, and Osiris makes a good father image. The pathworking is designed so that if someone has a poor mother image, he or she can choose Isis, and for a weak father image, he or she can choose Osiris. Before the pathworking begins, the person should be shown pictures of Osiris or Isis, so that the pathworker can be familiar with their form. After completing the pathworking, the pathworker is encouraged to say the word "Mother" if the goal was a Mother archetype, or "Father" if a Father archetype while visualizing the god or goddess. This builds up the association between the godform and the psyche.

Healing the Parental Archetypes Pathworking

Now relax, and regulate your breathing. I want to open your inner vision and imagine that you are a seven-year-old child in ancient Egypt. You are in a small bedroom with a primitive bed in one corner. This is your room. It is part of a great temple of (Isis or Osiris). The people of the village bought you here after your parents were swept away when the Nile burst its banks. You cannot remember your parents because you were a baby.

Today is the Festival of Orphans, where the children like you are presented to the (god or goddess) in the hopes of a blessing. You have put on your best robe and are waiting to be called to the temple.

You are nervous. This will mean that you will stand before the statue in front of all the priests, including the high priest, and selected people from the village. There is a gentle knock on the door and Khem, who has been teaching you how to write the complex hieroglyphs that make up the language of Egypt, opens it.

"They are ready for you now (insert your real name)," Khem says. Without a word, you follow Khem through the labyrinth of cool, whitewashed corridors and into the bright sunlight of the temple's courtyard. You hurry up the stairs to the temple and through the huge copper double doors. The temple is dark after the brightness of the courtyard, and the things you sense are the sweet smell of incense and the rattling of many sistrums.

As your eyes adjust to the gloom, you see priests and others lining the brightly painted columns of the temple. They are looking toward the golden curtain that seals off the Holy of Holies from the rest of the temple. Only the senior priests and priestesses go in that room, for that is where the statue of (Isis or Osiris) is placed, far from the eyes of the profane. Only on special holy festivals is the statue brought from its resting place.

You are led down the aisle, toward the golden curtain, to where the high priest is waiting. He is holding a wand in the shape of a lotus flower. You are a little frightened of the high priest because you have been told that he is the closest to the (god or goddess) in the whole of the temple. He looks at you with kindly eyes, and you relax.

The priestesses sing a hymn to (Isis or Osiris).

The high priest turns and raises his wand toward the curtain, and begins to chant the name of (Isis or Osiris). The chant is taken up by the choir, and this seems to make the whole temple vibrate with a special power.

You are aware of a presence behind the curtain—a living golden light.

The curtain parts, and before you in all (his or her) glory is (Isis or Osiris).

Everyone falls on their knees. You are drawn to meet the gaze of this being. (Isis or Osiris) looks directly at you. But (his or her) look does not bring fear, only a deep feeling of love, love that you felt long before you were born.

"(Insert your real name)," says the (god or goddess). "Your parents were taken from you by fate, and as a result, you are without an earthly (mother or father). That which is your blood and body is not the real you. You are a child of the stars, incarnating in a body of clay. Your true parents are the gods themselves, only most people forget it.

"You, who are without earthly parents to distract you, have the ability to realize your true parents and become the (son or daughter) of a (god or goddess). In the name of Amun, the Hidden One, I declare in front of this assembly that (your full name) is now my (son or daughter)."

There is a stunned shock in the temple. This is a great honor, as few have had the right to declare that they were the son or daughter of a god or goddess.

(Osiris or Isis) walks over to you and embraces you. There is a tremendous feeling of love, stability, and security. "Come with me, child of the gods," (he or she) says. (He or she) takes you by the hand and leads you into the Holy of Holies. This room is dark, lit by a single candle and the light radiating from the (god or goddess). On a simple altar is a life-sized statue of the (god or goddess).

"My image is a gateway to me. Whenever you see it, it will call me. Whenever you need courage, whenever you need love, whenever you need security, guidance, and support, all you need to is look upon this image and I will be with you. For I am your (mother or father), now and until the end of the age." Look into the eyes of the (god or goddess), and know that this is now your heritage and your future.

(Isis or Osiris) holds you in a deep and loving embrace. There is a joy that passes beyond time to this place and this reality. What was true in the pathworking is true now. (Insert your real name) is a true child of (Isis or Osiris). When you open your eyes, this will be so.

Healing for a Sexual Abuse Victim

Sexual abuse in any form leaves a heavy legacy, often for a lifetime. If the abuse happened in childhood, it can mar the chance of a committed relationship. Rape often brings feelings of fear and distrust to sexual and emotional partnerships. Counseling and other therapy does often enable a person to come to terms with the problem, particularly those feelings that somehow he or she is responsible for the assault.

There are few outlets acceptable to the victim that enables a feeling of justice to be done. Most rapes and sexual assaults are never reported, and those that do put the victim in an incredibly difficult position. Sometimes the attacker is another partner under whom the victim lives in total fear, and is unable to break free from. In other cases, it is parental sexual abuse, and the truth is so horrible that the memory of the event sometimes does not resurface until the attacker is dead. One of the things I have noticed about sexual abuse victims is that once the victims have the bravery to face the fact that they have been attacked, there is an incredible anger they feel, that their attacker has somehow succeeded in hurting them, ruining their lives, and that the attacks have went unpunished. This anger is the liberation of emotional energy from the emotional complex that has imprisoned it for years. The pent-up anger can last for years, leading to bitterness and a cynicism about life and relationships. Instead of healing, the person continues to be a victim, never mastering the situation. Sometimes these victims do have the strength to face their attackers in a courtroom. In my job as a reporter, I have seen many rape and sexual assault cases, and I can say that in a human court often nothing like justice is done. Even when the right person ends up behind bars, the victim feels that he or she has been through an ordeal, which doubles the sense of unfairness of the whole thing. It is a pity, for if the court case worked, then the result could be incredibly cathartic.

This pathworking is designed to open a channel between the victim and cosmic justice. Its message is that not only will the universe deal with any revenge that is required, but also it will correct any imbalance and allow the victim to move on with his or her life.

This pathworking is incredibly intense for the pathworker. The victim has to face his or her attacker to reactivate his or her pain, so the universe can take it away. For this reason, I suggest that the leading of the pathworking be performed by a nurturing group of people of the opposite sex of the victim's attacker, as there is always the risk that the pathworker will project his or her anger and fear onto the nearest target who is of the same sex as the pathworker's attacker.

The pathworking is based around the concept of universal justice as exemplified by the Egyptian goddess of justice Maat, who was considered so powerful that all life would have to come before her to be judged, including the other gods.

Healing for a Sexual Abuse Victim Pathworking

Allow yourself to relax as much as possible. Regulate your breathing, and allow these following images to appear in your mind's eye.

Before you is a curtain, upon which is a picture of a set of golden scales.

Concentrate on the curtain, and the scales will start to glow with power. The curtain parts, and standing before you is a being with a jackal head. This is Anubis. He says, "Why do you seek the Temple of Maat?"

You reply, "I have been wronged, and this wrong has created an imbalance that is against the rule of Maat. I seek justice so that balance may be restored."

Anubis replies, "All calls for justice in the temple of Maat are heard. Are you ready?"

If you agree, then the jackal-headed god will allow you to enter the gate. He says, "Enter thou then the halls of justice, the place of truth, the judgment hall of Maat."

You find yourself in a vast Egyptian temple. It is the color of flame.

Arranged in a semicircle before you are figures seated on thrones cut from red sandstone. They are dressed alike in kilts and nemyss of black and yellow. Some are human, but others are animals. Each wears a necklace in the shape of a flying hawk, and each carries a flail in their left hand. These are the forty-two assessors; the force of cosmic justice that even judges the gods.

In front of them is a giant pair of scales. Behind the scales is a beautiful woman. On the crown upon her head is the red feather of truth, which represents absolute truth. This woman is Maat; she is the force of cosmic balance, and just looking at her calms you further. This is a person to be trusted. Maat asks you slowly and quietly to tell the story of what happened to you. Starting at the beginning, you recount everything you can remember. The court is hushed as you tell your story.

Maat comes from behind the scales.

She says, "Every story has two sides. Therefore, we must also hear the person you have accused. Be aware that in this place no harm can come to you, for there is not a god nor demon who can withstand my power."

Then in a voice that commands the very atoms of life she says, "Bring forth the accused!"

A hawk-headed god enters. This is Horus, and he has a sword in his right hand. In his left hand he holds a thick chain attached to four dog-faced demons. Between them, also chained and looking tiny and impotent, is the accused. (He or she) looks at the scales with terror.

Maat approaches and asks the accused to patiently to explain (his or her) side of the story. In the halls of truth, it is impossible to lie. What does this person say?

Maat goes over to the accused and puts her hand deep into (his or her) chest. There is no blood, but she pulls out a ball of energy. This is the heart of the accused. Only in the hall of truth is this possible without the death of the person. She places the ball of light on one of the scales.

You have the impression that something is being decided. The forty-two assessors are telepathically debating the merits of the case with exact precision. They outstretch their arms, pointing their fingers toward the scales. The scales begin glowing with power.

Maat places the feather of truth upon the empty scales.

The scales sink on the side of the heart. The weight of the person's guilt is too heavy to support the truth. There is a rumbling as the ground shakes slowly.

"My rule has been shaken by this unbalanced act. It is necessary to restore it and make the victim whole again," says Maat.

She turns to the guilty person. "You, who have violated this fellow human and the rule of Maat, are now free from my protection. Those dog-faced demons are your violent aspects, bestial and untamed. These are what you release onto others, creating harm."

Taking the feather of truth, she touches each of the dog-faced demons in turn and then says to the guilty person, "Therefore, I have decided that each time these demons are released, they will attack only you. This will happen in this lifetime and will continue to happen until you master these demons. This is the will of Maat."

Maat throws the heart to the nearest demon, who eats it hungrily.

The chains fall from the demons and the guilty person. (He or she) flees the temple, closely followed by the demons who are biting at his or her heels.

Maat looks at you. "That is only part of the work of justice. Justice must be seen to heal the victim of the wrong that has been committed."

She leans into you and takes your heart. There is no pain, just a tingling. She places your on one of the scales and puts her feather of truth on the other. But unlike the last time when there was judgment, she holds the scales in your favor, slowly moving them so that they are in perfect balance with her feather.

"I who am the force of cosmic justice restore your heart to perfect balance and harmony," she says.

She returns your heart to you. You feel momentarily dizzy as your heart moves to restore all the energy centers to their proper balance.

She looks at you, "Know this, Child of Earth, that you are truly healed and the rule of Maat is established in your very body. Go now with my blessing and live your life in balance and truth."

Still a little groggy, you thank Maat and leave via the door though which you entered.

Finding the Center

In times of stress it is important to be able to center yourself and find that higher aspect of yourself. This will enable you to draw on the power of your own spiritual strength, giving you the courage to press ahead. This brief pathworking is designed to do just that. Although it appears simple, it is extremely powerful, particularly when performed over time. Its simplicity means that it can be easily memorized and practiced. Ideally, this pathworking should be practiced daily, as well as in times of stress.

Finding the Center Pathworking

Visualize yourself inside the golden sphere at your heart. Before you is a great red rose. A beam of light comes from above your head, down your spine, to connect to the rose, which slowly opens. You walk into the rose and there, in its center, is a black cubic altar. On the altar, in a small golden cup, is a single flame. This flame is your divine spark, the real you, which has built countless personalities throughout many incarnations. The flame is infinite, yet small and still. Commune with it. Feel it. Desire knowledge of it. Let the flame speak to you.

When you are finished, step back from the rose and see it close. Expand your consciousness to encompass the whole of your body. Feel the rose and its flame in your heart.

CHAPTER FIVE

Using Myth

Myths and legends contain many components that can be used in the construction of Inner Kingdoms or pathworkings. This is because they contain archetypal situations and powerful symbols that are essentially timeless. Encoded within the legends of its gods are formulas that, if unlocked by magical techniques, can lead to the total regeneration of the self. One such formula—taken from the Egyptian Book of the Dead—was the cornerstone of the Golden Dawn system of magic. In its initiations, candidates were bought into the magical myth of the "Judgment of Osiris" where their souls were judged by the forty-two assessors and awakened to the light of life. The Golden Dawn adepts in 1888 were even able to use the same legend as the basis for rituals that turned dead wood and metal into magical, living talismans. The "Judgment of Osiris" is a formula derived from one small part of a single legend. There were many different myths all with their own techniques and magical methods.

Carl Jung and Joseph Campbell both experimented extensively with myth as part of psychotherapy, and they were both convinced of the universality of all myths to reflect the unconscious mind. Some cultures place a subtly different emphasis on different aspects of archetypal symbols in accordance to their own worldview. For example, a tribe that has lived in a single valley for hundreds of years worships a tree at the mouth of the valley. This tree is believed to be a guardian to the afterlife, and spirits of the ancestors are said to land on its tops. Campbell would identify this tree as a representative of the World Tree, a gateway linking the underworld with heaven. The tribal priest would not say that; to him the tree is a place of fear because it stands on the path that leads to the outside world. The spirits that descend upon it are evil because they have not gone onto the afterlife. The tree does not reach heaven, only a form of purgatory.

In the Western Mystery Tradition, we use many myths as part of our inner work and rituals. I know of one ritual group that bases its entire ritual working on the legend of Gareth, who starts out as a squire on his way to King Arthur's court. During the group's magic ritual, the initiate symbolically becomes Gareth, and then the pathworking is read out loud. The result of this is that the initiate takes on the qualities of Gareth and learns his lessons as part of the curriculum of the group.

So powerful are these archetypes that sometimes they are renowned for biting the people who use them unwisely. For example, there was a Romano-British reenactment group I know of who adopted the titles of characters from the Arthurian myth as part of their performances. This worked well for a number of years until the person playing Lancelot ran off with the wife of "Arthur." There was general dissatisfaction with the way "Arthur" was running the group, so much so that more than half the group sided with "Arthur" while the rest sided with the person who called himself "Mordred." The situation grew very nasty until finally the group dissolved.

So, how is it possible to take the raw material of a legend and use it in a pathworking program? Obviously the body of mythology is vast, but for a case study this book will look at a single legend in the Egyptian mythos—that of Horus and Set. By looking at the approach adopted here, it will be possible to adapt any myths and legends into useful pathworkings. Let us look at the legend of Horus and Set first.

The Legend of Horus and Set[1]

Osiris was the greatest and most wise king, but his brother Set desired his kingdom. Set killed Osiris by cutting his body into many pieces and distributed them all over Egypt.

Osiris' wife and sister Isis gathered the severed parts of Osiris and joined them to make him whole again—all except the phallus, which had been swallowed by a fish. She built Osiris a replacement phallus of gold. Then, with her magic, she bought Osiris back to life for long enough to have sex. From that union she gave birth to their son Horus, who began a series of wars with Set for control of all the kingdoms.

From the moment of his birth, Horus has been at war with Set, and some say this battle has never been resolved. Horus suffered at Set's hands until he learned the arts of war. Then Set refused him battle, always preferring to strike when Horus was not ready and unable to bring his strength to bear. But finally after years of inconclusive war, Ra, the ruler of the gods, declared Set an outcast and rallied a massive army to fight him.

Set fled to Nubia and Ra floated his troops in barges down the Nile to do battle. At Thest-Hoor, Ra was joined by Horus Edfu, whose name means "harpooner and hero." It is said that Horus enjoyed fighting Set more than rejoicing.

Thoth, the god of magic and wisdom, appeared to Horus and gave him the ability to change himself into a great sun disk with sunset-colored wings. Thus Horus, as a great winged sun disk, sat on the prow of Ra's barge, his power flashed upon the waters of the Nile, and Horus sensed Set's army as they waited in ambush.

Horus rose into the air and, with a mighty burst of power, pronounced a powerful curse "Your eyes shall be blinded and ye shall not see. Your ears shall be deaf and ye shall not hear."

The Followers of Set were thrown into confusion. When a man saw his neighbor, he thought that he was looking at a stranger and their own language sounded foreign. Some killed each other, while the rest fled.

But the winged sun disk Horus was unable to find Set, who was hiding with his main army in the marshes of the north country. Horus returned and Ra gave him wine mixed with water—which is still poured as a libation to Horus Edfu.

Then the Followers of Set shapeshifted themselves, becoming crocodiles and hippopotami who can live underwater and whose thick skins can turn a sharp spear. They rushed upon the barge of Ra, seeking to overturn it. But Horus was ready for them.

Horus had ordered arrows and spears to be made with magical words and spells cast over them. When the fierce beasts came out of the water, the Followers of Horus let fly with their magical arrows and charged with their spears. The magic metal pierced the hides and reached the hearts of the wicked animals, killing 650 of them.

The rest fled; those who faced the south ran the fastest, for they were being chased by Horus Edfu and his followers. The Followers of Set were defeated twice near Denderah, Hathor's city. This was the end of Set's armies in the south. In the marshes of the north, Set and his followers waited; they had shapeshifted into crocodiles and lay hidden in the water.

Horus ordered his army to silence as they searched for four days and nights for Set's followers. On the fifth day, Horus found the ambush and he and his followers again routed his enemies. This time he bought back 142 prisoners to the barge of Ra.

The Followers of Set made for the north. When they came to the western waters of the Mert, where an ally of Set had his house, they stopped. Horus followed, but lost Set's army.

At the house of Rerhu, Ra told Horus where Set and his army were, and Horus marched his troops toward the rival army. They came to the point were the never-setting stars wheel around a certain point in the sky, and on the banks of Mert the battle began.

Again the Followers of Horus were victorious. Horus executed 181 of the prisoners in front of Ra's barge and gave their weapons to his followers. Now Set came out of his hiding place and he boasted he would destroy Horus. The wind bore the words of his boasting to Ra, who told Thoth to "cause these high words to be cast down." Horus attacked Set and his army. In the thick of the battle, Horus thought he had found Set. He bound his enemy's arms and tied his staff across him so that his enemy could make no sound, and placed his weapon at his foe's throat. Horus dragged the bound enemy back to Ra, who told him that Horus could do as he wished with his father's murderer. Horus struck the bound prisoner in the head, cutting him open to his back, and then Horus cut off the head and chopped the body into many pieces.

Thus Horus treated what he thought was Set's body, just as Set had treated his father' corpse. This took place on the first month of the season, when the flooding of the Nile recedes. But it was not Set whom Horus had killed, but an only an ally of Set. Set had changed himself into a mighty snake and entered into the earth. No one saw this, but since he was fighting against the gods, they were aware of what happened.

Horus waited in the barge of Ra for six days and six nights, waiting to see if there were any Followers of Set left—but they were all corpses on the water. Then Horus and his followers searched the two lands for his enemies, slaying 106 in the east and 106 from the west. These they slew before Ra in his sanctuaries.

Ra gave to Horus and his followers two cities, which are called the Mesen cities, for the Followers of Horus are *Mesenti,* the metal workers.

In the shrines of the Mesen, Horus is the god and his secret ceremonies are held on four days of the year.

Now the Followers of Set gathered together. Horus Edfu transformed himself into the likeness of a lion with the face of a man, with arms of green flint, and on his head was the Atef crown (which is the white crown of the northern kingdom) with the feathers and horns and on either side a crowned serpent.

Horus routed Set's army, which took to the Great Green Sea. Thoth calmed the waves of the ocean and the wind was lulled, but there was no enemy in sight. Horus' navy sailed around the coast of Africa until they came to Nubia, where he saw Set's followers gathered. Horus shapeshifted into a great winged disk, and on either side of him came the goddesses Nekbet and Uazet in their form of great hooded snakes with crowns upon their heads.

On Nekbet was the white crown on the south, while on Uazet was the red crown of the north. And the gods on the barge of Ra cried out, "See how Horus places himself between the two goddesses! Behold how he overcomes his adversaries!"

After the battle, the Followers of Set were routed. Ra—his boat moored at Thest-Hoor—ordered that on the main entrance to every temple in the two lands should be carved the winged sun disk with Nekbet and Uazet flanking it. After months and years, Set came forth and challenged Horus in the presence of Ra.

Horus came forth with his followers on their barges with their glittering armor and weapons with handles of worked wood and cords. Isis made golden ornaments for the prow of the barge and laid within it magic words and spells. Set took the form of a red hippopotamus and came from the south with his allies to meet Horus Edfu.

At the Elephantine the two armies met. Set stood up and spoke a great curse against Horus and Isis, saying, "Let there be a great wind and a raging tempest." At once, a storm broke over the barges of Horus and his followers. The wind roared and the water was lashed into great waves. But Horus held his way, and through darkness of the storm and the foam the waves gleamed from his great golden prow. Horus shapeshifted into the form of a young man eight cubits high, armed with a harpoon.

The blade of the harpoon was four cubits, the shaft was twenty cubits, and a chain of sixty cubits was welded to it. Horus held the weapon over his head as if it were a reed and threw it at Set, who was waiting in the deep waters for people to fall from Horus' barge. The harpoon pierced Set's brain and killed him.

Examining the Myth

Firstly, when you look at a myth, it is important to work out what the central theme is. Here we appear to have a myth about good versus evil, with an awful lot of fighting involved. On the face of it, this is a story of wars and battles between two gods and seems to have very little to do with magic.

Indeed, it seems likely that the story of the wars of Horus could be a legendary recounting of the battles between two historical factions—the Followers of Horus (the Shemsu Hor) and the Followers of Set (the Smayu Net Set). The Shemsu Hor drew its members from every district in Egypt—probably only those highly placed in the military and administration. In later years, the pharaoh's retinue and supporters were called the Shemsu Hor. Their symbol was the golden standard—a hawk. Of the Followers of Set there is less known; the Followers of Horus must have wiped them out if the legends are true.

In the Second Dynasty a member of the Followers of Set became pharaoh, taking the name Peribsen. This led to a split in the country between the Shemsu Hor and the Smayu Net Set, which was only resolved when Peribsen's successor Khasekhemwy attempted to heal the division by giving both Horus and Set equal importance.

There are elements to this legend that go beyond history, as it features magical elements like shapeshifting and archetypal symbols, which, if used magically, will result in transformation.

Transformation is achieved by the fusion of the lower self with the will of the Higher Self, and this is the first important goal of the magician seeking mastery of magic. It is not surprising that the home of alchemy, ancient Egypt, provides the techniques for transformation within its system of religious magic.

So, having uncovered the theme of transformation, we next start to pull apart the different aspects of the myth into their various components. The easiest way to do this is to meditate on each aspect of the myth and try to find a deeper meaning to what is going on.

In the legend of the wars between Set and Horus, we have to look for the many elements that show how it is a magical formula for transformation—both magically and psychologically—to remodel the self in the mold of its higher nature.

There are many different levels on which to read this legend. Psychologically, Horus represents the divine child; the true self that gradually becomes aware of its true nature. Set then is not only his personal shadow, but the darker aspects of his racial heritage. This is hinted at in the family tree of the gods in the legend. Set was Osiris' dark brother who was able to destroy him. Horus therefore inherited his father's shadow—the Judeo-Christian concept of the sins of the fathers being visited on the son. Initially, Horus is ill-equipped to face these sins and loses battles to Set.

This is indicative of the state when the newly awakened divine consciousness continues to try to follow the patterns of society and lower habit, resulting in the stunting of spiritual growth. Horus learns the arts of the warrior—he learns to fight against his environment and discipline himself against those things that stand in the way of development.

This is only the first stage. The young spiritual warrior finds himself continually at odds with the greater shadow. Sometimes he wins a

small victory, but mostly the shadow of Set strikes when he is least expected and injures Horus. It is only when the greater self—the Higher
Self, which is depicted in this legend by Ra, decides action must be
taken against the shadow that the war really begins in earnest.

So far, the emerging self having only arranged small skirmishes
with Set, now he meets up with the Higher Self and its legions to do
serious work that will free it, and a piece of humanity, from the
shadow's grip. This meeting happens at Thest-Hoor, whose name is derived from the Egyptian meaning of balance and halfway. The Higher
Self moves down the levels of spirit and meets the ascending aspiring
personality halfway. It is a state represented by the symbol of the hexagram or a Star of David with its two interlocking triangles: one pointing up and the other down. Horus is often depicted carrying a spear
guarding the prow of Ra's barge. Ra is behind him, but Horus carries
out all the fighting in the legend.

This is a partial integration of the aspiring personality with its
higher aspects. It is familiar to most occultists who have reached the
level known as "knowledge and conversation with the holy guardian
angel." In this, the higher personality telepathically communicates with
the lower either in the form of dreams, inspirations, or with a "still,
clear" voice. In common terms, this is the voice of the conscience.
Horus is given the power to transform himself into a sun disk by the
god Thoth. This is an interesting stage in development, because it
shows a degree of difficulty for the personality to accept its own divine
nature. Communication between the Higher Self and the lower self is
still not clear enough for important specifics to be passed down, because the lower self still sees itself as separate from the Higher Self.

So the Higher Self calls upon an aspect of itself with whom the
lower self can communicate. This is the doctrine of the masters, or highly
evolved beings or gods, who are often seen assisting a personality to the
light. In this case, Horus' Thoth contact teaches him how to build an astral vehicle that will enable Horus to ascend the levels and deal with the

shadow at a more profound level. The winged sun disk symbol, which yields much to meditation, is a link to the divine self and brings with it some of the Higher Self's magical powers.

The first time Horus ascends, he sees the Followers of Set waiting in ambush and pronounces a curse against them, which prevents them from seeing or hearing. Horus magically breaks down the cohesive power of the shadow by forcing each follower or "sin" to stand alone so that it can be destroyed. This is very successful, but can only be partial because some aspects of the shadow reside in complexes too deep for Horus to approach at this time. Although this legend is smeared with violence, death, and killing, this violence is only trappings to appeal to the child-like mind of the lower self; after all, legends were written for the immature mass mind.

The ancient Egyptians had a strong belief in the afterlife and saw death, whether by war or natural causes, as a transformation from one life to another. In using psycho-magical techniques, nothing is killed, it is just transformed into something more useful. After Horus' first victory, the way is clear for the Higher Self to reward Horus with wine and water. Wine, in this case, is a symbol of the blood, and its dilution refers to a refinement and purification of the life force contained within the blood.

It is said that the blood of the adept is more refined than an ordinary person's. This is one of the reasons why the legends of Atlantis talk of breeding programs, where priests and kings were not allowed to mate outside their caste in order to keep the bloodlines pure. This refined blood activates other physical centers, which enables the aspiring self to ascend still further. It is this gift of Ra that enables Horus to start on the next stage of his training, which is to refine and perfect the metallic substances in his body and aura, so that they can be used as weapons against the shadow.

This is the work of alchemy, which in its initial stages means the refining of the elements within the personality rather than transmutation. Thus Horus is seen forging metal weapons and chanting magical words into their composition. Magically, this represents the magician working with the planetary forces to enable them to become clear channels through the personality. The battle at this point is with the negative aspects ascribed to planetary influences.

It has been said that it is impossible to change the stars and you have to live with their positive and negative effects. Yet, by the refining the positive aspects of the planets using planetary alchemy, Horus defeat Set's followers yet again.

There are now two battles around Denderah, the city of Hathor. Cow-headed Hathor was the ultimate mother goddess, often associated with the heavens, and was the female counterpart to Thoth. Horus at this point is dealing with the creative aspects of himself—he is discovering the Mother.

Although this version of the legend does not mention it, later versions speak of Isis actually helping Set defeat her son. Reducing the legend to a human relationship, where a shadow is allowed to develop to the extent that it destroys one partner and carries on into another generation, the surviving partner must shoulder some of the blame for failing to help destroy the shadow. Worse, the surviving partner must also accept responsibility for passing that sin on to the other generations.

This is clearly true in the extreme case of physical and sexual abuse, which is a problem that passes through generations. It takes two battles to deal with this issue, and finally this brings to an end the war for Upper Egypt (or the unconscious). Set did not really dwell in Upper Egypt; all these battles were just clearing up the subjective results of the shadow.

Now it is time for Horus and the armies of Ra to meet the shadow in its more tangible aspects. In the war for the north of Egypt, much time is spent trying to find the enemy. There are no longer any subjective results to look for, so a problem is harder to locate and tackle. Horus manages to find Set the first time by ordering his army to silence. Like the quieting of the self that is carried out in meditation, Horus stills himself entirely.

This is not the sort of meditation that Horus had previously practiced, which was more active, it is the deeper meditation that the Zen Buddhists have mastered, where all aspects of the self are brought to calm. Now Horus can still the unconscious so that it provides a near perfect reflection of the astral worlds above.

In doing so, he encounters the first armies of the Followers of Set and defeats them. This is the first time we hear of Horus taking prisoners after a battle, because the powers that previously had done him no good can be used in a positive way if turned to their correct purpose. This is why Horus brings them to the Higher Self, here represented by Ra, to see if they should be integrated.

The Followers of Set retreat further, hoping to escape to the Great Green Sea (the collective unconscious). They stop at the house of one of Set's followers on the banks of Mert. This represents a major complex—for Mert was feminine and represented the night.

One of the Mert goddesses was Set's estranged wife—Nepthys. She had slept with Osiris, giving birth to Anubis, perhaps suggesting a shadow aspect of Isis. Horus once again cannot find the Followers of Set, but at the house of Rertu (who was a hippopotamus goddess associated with Set) Ra tells him where to find them.

This is another time that the Higher Self steps in to clearly advise when the lower self has run out of ideas. Horus, because of his victories in the south, knows the effects of a corrupted Mother image. By approaching it in its higher aspects, Horus is able to come to terms with the Mother image enough to face it properly.

This battle takes place where "the never-setting stars wheel around a certain point in the sky." It is a place of stillness where Horus discovers the horrors of a corrupted Mother image and sees its projections on the zodiac of his life. Horus has ceased to deal with the problem piecemeal and returns to the center of his being to deal with the root cause.

In the battle, Horus captures "prisoners" and takes them to Ra. This time the "prisoners" cannot be controlled and Horus kills them. But he does take their weapons: in other words, he transmutes their ability to hurt him into the more useful project of destroying the shadow.

Now Set himself comes forth. This is the great personal shadow, the dweller on the threshold, who is now nearing the end of his rulership. However, Set is still confident and boasts that he will destroy Horus. He is using the power of words, which framed in a particular way can bring about new images of destruction on the lower self.

This time the Higher Self, in its Thoth aspect, intervenes to stop Set in creating new images, enabling the battle to be fought fairly. If left to itself, the consciousness will make more mistakes and program the lower self with new complexes. In this case, the higher magical aspect of the self can assist by stopping these faulty images before they start creating new ones.

Through ritual, meditation, or pathworking techniques, it is possible to neutralize the creation of new and faulty complexes. In the final battle, Set is captured by Horus. Set's arms are bound and Horus has tied his staff over his mouth so that he cannot speak. In other words, Horus has neutralized his personal shadow through willpower.

By the time of this last battle with the personal Set, Horus is equipped magically to deal with his own shadow. When he appears, Horus can silence this shadow. Horus takes his shadow to Ra, who says that Horus can do what he likes with Set. Once this victory is accomplished, the dweller on the threshold in his current form is of no use to anything, so Horus kills him and hacks the body into as many pieces as Set had done to Osiris. Set at this point becomes an Osiris, a symbol of life and rebirth.

The legend is hinting that the shadow has begun the slow process of integration with the rest of the personality. This was enacted ritually when the floodwaters of the Nile pulled back to reveal the fertile land. It is the point where the adept (to use Golden Dawn terminology) has crossed the boundaries between the outer and inner order. Now he begins to work magic for humanity, rather than himself, and seeks to damage Set in the wider world.

The legend reveals that Set has not been killed after all. Set is a cosmic force and cannot be killed as such. Horus has purged Set from the little bay that is his personality—but mankind has a shadow, too, and it is this greater Set who must be faced by the adept. In the legend, this greater Set turns himself into a snake and enters the earth.

The Higher Self is aware of this and, while the lower self rejoices at his newfound integration, warns him that the war is not yet over. This comes as a shock to the lower self because until this point it has been allowed to see itself as separate from the rest of humanity.

Now, if it is going to personally proceed, the Higher Self's destiny lies with helping humanity to deal with Set. New armies of Set begin to appear, perhaps because of self-doubt at the greatness of this task and the pressures on the lower self now to integrate. Horus, however, in his meditative state is able to destroy these niggles with newfound power.

He searches the two lands for minor complexes that stand in the way of total integration with the Higher Self. This is what is indicated when Horus slew the Followers of Set before Ra in his sanctuaries. Horus has now achieved unity. Ra gives him two cities, both of which are connected to metalworking.

This gift links Horus to the arts of metal alchemy, the secrets of which Horus now perfects to take on the next stage of the Great Work. Ra seems to almost disappear from the legend at this point, as do most of the gods—other than Set and Thoth (who represents Horus' magical aspects). This is because Horus (the lower self) is so integrated with Ra (the Higher Self) that they cease to become separate identities. They are the two triangles of the hexagram—two that are one. (This is the work of the grade that the Golden Dawn referred to as Adeptus Minor.)

Dion Fortune described this experience as when the person becomes an initiate. We now begin to see Horus shapeshifting. The first form he uses is the image of a lion with arms of green flint, and a man's face wearing the Atef crown (the white crown of Upper Egypt flanked by two horns and two feathers). The lion is an alchemical symbol that stands for natural power; the raw, sexual power of the lower self. By having a human head, this indicates that Horus is now able to place this power under his will and is able to project it outward. The green flint arms represent the ability to remove the fire from the natural kingdom of earth and bring it forth. This is a hint that natural power, represented by the lion, draws its force from the earth.

W. E. Butler said that this power comes directly from the planetary being and the Earth's heart. The heart of this power was often depicted as being emerald green, and could be the prototype for the green stone of the Grail legends.

The Atef crown symbolizes the state of consciousness of the adept. The two feathers indicate that this rule of the Inner Kingdom is attained by balance, personified by the goddess Maat, whose symbol is a feather. The two horns indicate Hathor, the unconscious mind (represented in the tarot by the High Priestess card), which has been stilled and raised upward toward the divine. The crown's twin serpents are similar to the Greek caduceus, and represent the natural energies rising upward to merge with the one. (Mastery of this force can be obtained by meditating on the crown and the form of Horus with a lion's body and the head of a young boy. Bear in mind that this is a point where the Higher Self is totally identified with the lower self.)

The series of battles Horus is fighting at this point in the legend are still fairly close to his own self. It is the evil Horus sees in his own immediate environment. Set and his followers have escaped to the Great Green Sea, which as described earlier, represents the collective unconscious. In this turbulent mass it is much harder to find the root causes of complexes.

To remedy this problem, Thoth calms the waves to enable Set's navy to be seen. This is the effect that an initiate has on the mass mind, the peacemakers, to whom Jesus Christ referred in his Sermon on the Mount. The effect is to reveal the deeper problems and complexes of the mass mind so that they may be corrected. The stillness fails to reveal the forces of Set, who have long since fled deep into the aspects of the lower mass mind. They are unable to immediately affect the life of the two lands, but in the long term they can repair and return.

Horus and Ra sail around Africa searching for the armies of Set and finally locate him in Nubia (the deepest aspect of the mass mind). Horus uses a very highly powered technique to destroy the armies. He shapeshifts into the winged sun disk with the twin snake gods Nekhbet and Uazet, wearing their red and white crowns, flanking him. Previously in his form of a lion with a human face, Horus has used the earth power to destroy the Set beasts. Now he becomes an embodiment of that power, the Solar Logos, or intelligence, using the powers of the land.

At the legend's end, Set's influence has all but been removed from humanity, and Horus is given his rewards. The battles are far from over, as Horus must face Set again at the end of the great cosmic cycle. In those times Set will challenge humanity's rights in the presence of the cosmic Ra, and humanity will come forth armed with the weapons of its experience, our bodies glowing with the power of spiritual alchemy. The aspects of our collective unconscious will buffet us for the last time, but we will overcome it. Set will rise up and will be transmuted by us, so that we will become the vision of the One for which we were intended.

Imaginative Techniques Derived from the Legend

Having pulled apart a legend as much as possible, now it is time to work out ways use the magical power of the imagination to bring it to life. The following are two magical techniques that have been developed using the legend of the battles of Horus.

A reader could, without too much difficulty, develop pathworkings, or rituals, using other parts of the legend. The first pathworking I have written is designed to transmute part of the personality so that it can overcome a particular complex. The pathworking should be used at the climax of any personality work into a particular problem or habit.

This is a "lighter" version of the technique that we used in the last chapter. Unlike that one, however, the pathworking is not personalized and relies on the psychic pressure caused by the legend's symbolism to bring about change. The effect is to plant a suggestion deep into the unconscious and, on another level, to show the self a new reality.

What is unusual about this particular pathworking is that it incorporates a technique called *godform working*. A magician using a godform seeks to unify with the power and images that the godform represents. In this case, the magician so strongly identifies with Horus Edfu that he or she will seek to destroy the Set beast and not succumb to it. The godform will supply powers that are above the personality at that time.

Horus' Spear Pathworking

Sit comfortably in a chair with your feet flat on the ground. Shift your attention to the Yesod center, which is at the groin area. See it as a ball of vibrating, spinning, violet light. Imagine a six-inch statue of the god Horus Edfu forming at the center of this light. See it as hawk-headed armor-clad, holding a large spear.

Now imagine that high above your head is the star Sirius. Visualize a beam of light coming from that star, through the top of your head, down your spine, and connecting with the statue. See the statue come alive, breathe, and grow until it is just about as tall as your nose.

Then slowly enter into the mind of the god Horus Edfu until you feel that you are the mighty god. Look with his eyes, hear with his ears, for now you are Horus.

Figure 8: Horus Edfu

Visualize the following scene. Before you is a pylon gate of pink sandstone with a winged sundisk across its top lintel. On the other side is the mystical land of Khem—Egypt—the land of the legend.

Drawing a deep breath, you walk through the door into a sea of silver mist.

The mist clears and you are standing on the fertile eastern banks of the Nile. It is a hot morning, and there is not a cloud in the sky.

You feel that it is just the sort of day for an adventure, and you and your followers are planning an expedition to find one. You are saluting the sun with your spear when you hear the drums of approaching ships. It is a war fleet.

Excitedly, you look down the Nile to see banks upon banks of ships navigating their way up the river. Their sails are of gold and all bear the device of the hawk-headed sun god Ra.

Leading the flotilla is the mighty barge of Ra, and you strain your eyes to see the mighty god on his throne at the rear of his barge.

The sight takes your breath away, but the image brings with it a feeling of sadness, for Ra and you share the same symbol but he is mighty and all powerful, and you are just a refugee from your uncle's attacks.

"Where are they going?" you wonder, for this is the sort of adventure that you would like to join. You rush to your followers, who are making ready your barge for your hunting trip. You bid them to hurry and together you push your barge into the water.

You originally intend to join the wings of the flotilla, but much to your surprise you see a signal from Ra's flagship signalling you come along side. With some steering you navigate your tiny barge into the shadow of the mighty flagship. Then there is another signal. Ra wants you and your followers to come onboard.

Your mind is a whirl as you run your barge alongside the ship and throw mooring ropes to draw you alongside. A ladder is lowered over the side of the flagship and you climb. As you emerge over the side of the boat you find your feet on rich pink and gold carpet. Your eyes are instantly drawn to the might golden throne that towers above the deck.

Sitting on the throne, masked in a great golden hawk's mask, is Ra. You bow before him. You notice at his feet is a magnificent spear that seems to glow with magical power. You rise to look at him but Ra does not say a word. "My Lord Ra cannot speak with you at this time," says a voice gentle as a summer wind.

You look up and see the ibis-headed god Thoth. In his hands he holds an ankh. "However, he bids me to ask you to stand your guard in the prow of his boat. Is this acceptable to you?"

Figure 9: Thoth

You eagerly nod and ask, "Who is my lord's enemy that he shall be my enemy?"

Thoth replies. "Our enemy is indeed thine—for it is the slayer of your father Osiris, your uncle Set, whom we seek to kill." Your hand instinctively tightens around your spear at the mention of your uncle's name.

"It would give me great pleasure to help Ra in his quest, for indeed revenge for my father's death has been my goal from before I was born," you tell Thoth. You bow and take the place of honor at the prow of Ra's barge.

Hours pass with nothing happening but the sound of water rushing against the prow of the barge. You remain alert, for you know that your uncle will only attack when you least expect it. Then your sharp eyes see it a mile off.

A crocodile?

No, something much bigger.

A hippopotamus? Much bigger.

Then it dawns on you. It is something that has always frightened you. A nameless beast that your Uncle Set used to frighten you with when you were small.

You grip your spear and yell a warning to the fleet. The warning is shouted along the fleet and you see warriors grabbing their bows and arrows.

Yes, good, you think. *Kill the thing before it can get close and sink our barges.*

At your command, your warriors send wave after wave of arrows at the creature. The arrows seem to be turned long before they get to the beast. Invisible shields of energy smash the arrows aside before they get close.

The creature does not seem to want to move, but bars the way for the fleet.

"How do we kill something that cannot be killed?" you say to yourself out loud.

"We make a special weapon," says a voice and you turn to see Thoth.

"What weapon can get through the many shields that creature has?" you ask.

"With something like this," says Thoth, and in his hands he holds Ra's spear. Before you can take it, he says, "Each spear belongs to the man who must cast it. It becomes magically empowered by every evil that is killed. You must make your own magic spear, Horus."

You reply, "But how? I don't even know metalworking skills."

Thoth says: "I, who am the teacher of all things, shall teach you."

Ra orders the fleet to moor at the side of the river, and you and Thoth leave the barge. You walk along a path until you come to a wayside temple. Over the door is the winged sun disk.

Thoth tells you to take from the temple a vessel of holy water. As you enter, you find yourself in a tiny room. At one end is a statue of your mother Isis and in her lap is a silver bowl of water.

With a courteous nod to your mother's statue, you take the water and join Thoth. Before him is a great ladle, a mighty hammer, and a cube stone anvil.

Then, together, you gather wood into a pile for the fire. "Not too much, hawk fledgling," says Thoth, "for this fire needs no fuel."

You ask, "Then why have any wood at all?"

"There must be some kind of sacrifice for the divine fire to touch earth," replies Thoth.

Once the fire is ready, Thoth lifts his arms toward the sun and calls a mighty name of power. Note what this name is. A ray of sunlight strikes the wood. You notice that the fire does not burn; it just seems to dwell there turning the wood white-hot.

"Where are we going to get the magical metal to smelt?" you ask.

Thoth smiles and reaches into your body. It does not hurt, it just tickles. He takes his hand out and opens it, and you see a ball of metal about the size of a fist. Note what type of metal that Thoth is holding.

Thoth tells you to place the metal into the ladle and the ladle into the heart of the divine fire. Soon the metal has melted, but the top of it is covered with a black crust. You scrape the crust from the top of the metal and throw it into the heart of the fire, where it burns to nothing.

Taking the ladle from the fire, you pour the molten metal into the water. The water steams and the metal explodes, but becomes hard before it can escape the water.

The metal is contorted into a strange shape that reminds you of one of the Followers of Set, but as you wash the ingot in the holy water, it becomes totally clean and pure. Now the metal is purified. It is time to make ingot into a spear point.

Thoth takes Ra's spear and pushes the blade into the ground to form a mold. Then you melt the ingot again in the fire. This time when the metal is clear, bright, and glows with a rainbow of colors. Then Thoth teaches you a chant to sing to the metal that is within the flame. This may be a word of power, or it may be a vibration, but after a while the metal starts to boil with a new light. You pour the shining liquid metal into the hole in the ground made by Ra's spearpoint. The metal bubbles for a minute and then darkens as it cools and hardens.

You dig the spearhead from the earth and hold it to the light. You are disappointed because it is only roughly spear shaped. As if detecting your disappointment, Thoth smiles. "What, fledgling, you think that a magical spear can be made without work?" He gives you a hammer and tells you to beat the spearhead into shape. You hold the spear point in the sacred flame to warm it, place it upon the cubic forge, and then strike it hard.

Bang! With each strike of the hammer, Thoth recites a litany of names of power—some are of gods, others you do not know, but soon the vibration of these names starts to affect you.

Bang! The names seem to be passing through you, down the hammer and being stamped on the spearhead.

Every now and then you quench the spearhead in the water and start over again. Soon the spear point is bright and as sharp as a razor. More than that, it seems to glow with power. Taking your old spear you remove its spearhead and cast it into the sacred fire.

Then you place the new spearhead on the old staff. Thoth seems to grunt with satisfaction and you think that your spear looks much better than Ra's original. The pair of you board the barge, and at Ra's command the fleet moves toward the waiting Set fiend, with you standing at the prow of the boat, your spear at the ready.

The Set fiend seems to sense your presence and this time turns to attack. Closer and closer it comes, foam spraying outward from its limbs.

You see teeth, dark red eyes, and for a brief moment you are gripped by a fear. You realize that you are on the peripheries of the beast's shields and you are starting to feel its power.

Its head comes out of the water spraying foam, its jaws speaking of death and destruction to the fleet. You aim your spear and cast it toward the foul head with all the strength in your body. The spear sings as it leaves your hands.

The creature's shields move like tentacles to snatch the spear from the air, but the spear just passes through them. The spear hits the creature between the eyes and it lets out a mighty bellow, a thousand screams of fear, pain, tears, and terror. Images come rushing to your mind, incidents from your current life, each charged with emotion and power.

Then you discover the nature of the beast you have killed and the power you have released. The beast dissolves into thin air and the world is quiet again.

There is a buzzing noise and instinctively you lift your hand in front of your face. You clasp your spear, for somehow it has returned to you. You look at the spear tip. It is clean it is as if the beast had never been struck. As you hold the spear, you realize that it has more power than before. It is glowing with the magic that the Set fiend had imprisoned in itself.

You turn to face Ra and bow. Ra raises his scepter of power and says, "Behold Horus Edfu. Mighty is he, slayer of the Set beast. Surely shall he inherit his father's kingdom."

You have won a small victory in a big war, but from this victory you have the key to win other battles. Before you is the pylon gate. You step through it and into this time and place.

You sit in your body and visualize the statue of Horus Edfu shrinking. See the beam of light from Sirius free itself from the statue and your body. See the statue shrink until it is a speck and the center of Yesod stops spinning and grows dim. Be aware of your own body and personality. It is a personality that has been re-formed by the victory of Horus.

The Winged Sun Disk

The purpose of this pathworking is to ascend above emotional problems and see life as it really is. It is like a miniature version of the Inner Kingdom working that we looked at in chapter 2. With practice, it is possible to see the people you associate with, your workmates, and your family from a hawk-like perspective.

You will see people operating within a symbolic framework that should not be taken too literally, however, it will enable you to see where people are coming from, where they are going, and how they will influence your life. With skill from this exercise, it is possible while talking to someone to rise above the situation and see where he or she is coming from. It should also be possible to start seeing things that are coming up in your own life and problems that you will be expected to face.

Keep a record of your visions. When you start to notice that they are "proving true," start acting on them.

The process:

1. Perform the middle pillar exercise (see chapter 6).

2. Focus on a sphere of light above your head. Equate that with infinite divine power.

3. Draw down power, like you would in a middle pillar exercise, but stop it in the midbrain area.

4. See this light spiral into a sphere that fills your brain with power. Move your consciousness so that you are sitting within this sphere.

5. In your mind's eye, place your hands over your face and see them slowly turn into wings. The wings should be the color of sunset—turquoise, carnelian, and lazuli, shot with gold.

6. Stretch out your wings, move and flap them so that the disk of fire in which your consciousness is placed begins to ascend.

7. Feel your emotions and automatic mind fall away as you rise upward.

8. What is immediately below you is your personal world. You see people and inner world beings that are important to you. Farther away from you are distant friends, associates, and contacts who are of less importance to you at the moment.

9. Watch the way these people interact. What symbols are attached to them? What is happening to them?

10. If you want to have a close-up view of a person or situation, see an Eye of Horus appear before your face and look through it.

11. Look at the body of yourself. What is happening to you? What needs to be done?

12. When you are finished, sink back down into your body. Close the wings about your face. Let the light withdraw to the crown center.

13. Perform a cabbalistic cross (see chapter 6).

The winged sun disk exercise has many magical uses ranging from long-distance communication, healing, to self and interpersonal discovery. My own experience in this technique has proved to me that it is very effective at neutralizing the emotional clouds that prevent you making a decision at a time of crisis.

CHAPTER SIX

Imagination as a Mystical Tool

Throughout this book, we have looked at the use of imagination to access mental, emotional, and psychological states of consciousness. There is another state of consciousness that so far has only been hinted at. This is because its use has been a heavily veiled secret in the various mystical and magical schools. I am talking about the use of imagination to actually contact the divine.

When I say a veiled secret, some aspects of the various techniques to contact the divine have been published, usually by those who have stumbled across them as part of their mystical experiences rather than by occult training. Specific mention of the use of imagination in attaining these mystical states is usually only mentioned obliquely rather than using anything specifically.

Earlier I said that the Inner Kingdoms that we access in our imaginations are real and that our imagination is not so much creating them as using its vision to see them. If this is true of our own physiological, emotional, and mental states, it must also be true of the higher spiritual realms that are behind them. I would go further and say that it is extremely hard to experience spiritual states without the language of imagination to understand them. If you look at any documented religious experience, it is usually packed full of imagery that had meaning in the mind of the person who experiences it.

Take, for example, the religious experiences of the biblical prophet Ezekiel, who experienced angels and a vision of God. The following passages are packed full of imaginative symbolism.

> And I looked, and, behold, a whirlwind came out of the north, a great cloud, and a fire infolding itself, and a brightness was about it, and out of the midst thereof as the color of amber, out of the midst of the fire.
>
> Also out of the midst thereof came the likeness of four living creatures. And this was their appearance; they had the likeness of a man. . . . And I saw as the color of amber, as the appearance of fire round about within it, from the appearance of his loins even upward, and from the appearance of his loins even downward, I saw as it were the appearance of fire, and it had brightness round about.
>
> As the appearance of the bow that is in the cloud . . . so was the appearance of the brightness round about. This was the appearance of the likeness of the glory of the Lord. And when I saw it, I fell upon my face, and I heard a voice of one that spake.[1]

Here we can see fire, whirlwinds, clouds, and angels, and even that most evocative of symbols, the rainbow. This is material that could easily find its way into a pathworking. The Bible is packed with symbolism. Therefore, it is not surprising to find techniques much like pathworking being used by mystics that use the Bible as their main source.

The founder of the Jesuits, the Counter Reformation's champion, St. Ignatius of Loyola (1491–1556), had members of his order visualize the life of Christ. Ignatius had a month-long program for the members of his order, called the Spiritual Exercises. These worked much in the way of a modern esoteric schools' correspondence course. Each week a Jesuit would be required to perform these pathworkings, which were designed to enable the Jesuit to key into the thinking of St. Ignatius and to have spiritual experiences.

As a Jesuit, in the second week you would build your "imaginary" kingdom based on a visualization of the villages and towns where Christ lived. Then you would equate that kingdom with a good, wise, contemporary ruler. Then you would attempt to link that king with Christ as ruler.

In the third week you would visualize the life of Christ's final days through to the Last Supper. And, finally, in the fourth week you would visualize Christ's death and resurrection.

It is important to realize that the Spiritual Exercises would have a person watching the scene and contemplating its symbolism. The esoteric pathworking would have the same person interacting with the characters, feeling that they really were there. In my view, these exercises would have allowed for an intellectual understanding of a spiritual event, but may have stood in the way of a true spiritual awakening.

Closer to the esoteric schools is the mystic St. Teresa of Avila (1515–1582). In her book *The Interior Castle,* the central technique was much more hands-on. It is a journey through a "diamond" castle of the soul, with the goal being the center of the building to attain union with God.

"You must not imagine these mansions as arranged in a row, one behind another, but fix your attention on the centre, the room or palace occupied by the King. Think of a palmito, which has many outer rinds surrounding the savoury part within, all of which must be taken away before the centre can be eaten. Just so around this central room are many more, as there also are above it."[2]

St. Teresa's castle is broken down into seven mansions or rings.

First Mansion

This is where a person begins to meditate, but is still attached to the outside world. It is a period of humility and the beginning of discipline.

Second Mansion

This is where the person desires closer contact with God and actually starts to work hard at moving forward in the practice of meditation and prayer.

Third Mansion

Exemplary life begins as the person has attained virtue, and is controlled by discipline and penance and disposed to performing acts of charity toward others. He or she still lacks the full inspiring force of love, as love is still governed by reason. The person suffers from aridity.

Fourth Mansion

Mystical life begins as the person realizes it is not by the effort of the personality that the soul gets what it needs. The soul is seen like a fountain built near its source and the water of life flows into it, not through an aqueduct, but directly from the spring. Love is now free from servile fear: it has broken all the bonds that previously hindered its progress; it shrinks from no trials and attaches no importance to anything to do with the world.

Fifth Mansion

This is a very close contemplation of God. The faculties of the soul are "asleep." It is of short duration, but, while it lasts, the soul is completely possessed by God.

Sixth Mansion

If the fifth mansions were a betrothal, then in the sixth the lover and beloved see each other for long periods at a time, and as they grow in intimacy, the soul receives increasing favors, together with increasing afflictions.

Seventh Mansion

The soul has a spiritual marriage with God, and is transformed.

The irritating thing about *The Interior Castle* is that St. Teresa does not give us specific images of what a person might expect to see in each room, leading some to suggest that it is simply a metaphor and she is not actually doing anything like the magical use of the imagination. St. Teresa could not help but slip into some very beautiful imagery when describing her castle. Why would someone go the lengths to describe it as a diamond or a crystal if it were simply an allegory, not meant to be seen by the inner eye? Certainly those mystical friends of mine who use St. Teresa's castle do visualize it as a "physical" reality. My own experience with it was that I was taken to various rooms in each ring of the castle by a guide and led to understand certain spiritual ideas. In one instance, I tried to advance deeper into the castle than I was ready for. The light of the room was overwhelming and I had a sudden nosebleed, which snatched me out of the meditative reverie. Oddly, years later, I tried the same thing with no ill effects, so my spiritual knowledge must have improved since the last visit, or deity had kindly decided then to let me see.

Now we have looked at the public presentations of mystical imagination, it is time to look at the more occult versions.

The Difference Between Mystics and Occultists

Before embarking on looking at the use of imagination for mystical experience, it is important to get a definition of "mystic" and "occultist." Like the mystical writer and scholar R. A. Gilbert, I think that finding a definition that is neither grandiose nor limp is impossible. Quoting Evelyn Underhill, who believed that mysticism is the art of union with reality, Gilbert says that a mystic"is seeking to unite his whole soul, the core of his being with the Divine."[3] Definition is difficult, as a mystical experience is something that is often unique to all people. However, many people talk about it as a union with deity. Sometimes mystical experiences happen to those who are not looking for them. An agnostic friend of mine once had an overwhelming mystical experience when riding her bicycle in the New Zealand countryside. It had no spiritual effect on her life other than to lead her to question her notion of reality more.

Similar experiences with other people might have caused a change of life patterns. The classic case of this is Paul of Tarsus on his way to persecute Christians and suddenly being blinded by a divine light that lead him ultimately to Christianity. A mystic would say that such experiences bought without any personal efforts were rare and the product of divine grace.

Mystical experiences do not have to be dramatic, blinding lights either. They often are small steps that have dramatic consequences for the soul. My move away from orthodox Christianity was one such experience. In meditation at a Christian camp, I opened my eyes and saw the camp all around me, and it felt like a two-dimensional image of a divine reality that was actually many dimensions. All around I saw swirling shapes that suggested that the pattern of the universe was more complex and exciting than I could perceive with my religion. There must be more to God than this, I thought and resolved to find it. Yet, with this awakening came an inner calm and excitement. It was the sort of the feeling of the tarot Fool embarking on a quest.

Ultimately, both the mystic and the occultist are looking to achieve the same thing, either by a direct route in the case of the mystic or by the slower, less direct method of the occultist. Both occultists and mystics report the same essential experiences: a feeling of dying and being reborn, seeing light, experiencing union, and a feeling of total liberation. Generally, mystical experience starts with some fairly basic realizations. The first is that there is more to life than appears in physical reality. Most mystics would consider this reality the divine being. They would say that this divine being pervades everything but somehow remains out of reach of the ordinary consciousness and certainly is unknowable. Some identify this divine being with a divine aspect of themselves; others consider that the divine being is somehow separate and that a true mystical experience is a marriage between the divine being and themselves.

It has been said that all occultists end up as mystics in the end, but that is only after a different journey. Although there are similarities between the goals of the mystic and the occultist, their methods for getting to the same destination and what happens when they reach it are two different matters. Mystics will often sacrifice their participation in the world to attain this union at a higher level. They seek to "be in the world but not of it." Their path is of nonattachment, removal of the ego, never working for personal gain, i.e., a gradual stripping away of everything that is not the divine) until they find the part that is. Once this is attained, there is only this unity to bask in.

The sixteenth-century Spanish mystic St. John of the Cross (1542–1591) said, "When thy mind dwells upon anything, thou art ceasing to cast thyself upon the All."[4]

Mystics have travelled so lightly to reach their goal that there is nothing more that that can be done once they arrive, other than live the reminder of their life in a state of bliss and hope that others will be helped by contact with them.

Mystics will try to divorce themselves from too much use of symbol and imagination because these will become an attachment and a distraction from their ultimate direction. As the great fifteenth-century Catholic mystic Thomas ‡ Kempis said, "Shut fast the door of your soul—that is to say your imagination—and keep it cautiously, as much as you can, form beholding any earthly thing, and then lift up your mind to your Lord, Jesus; open your heart faithfully to Him,"[5] whereas occultists will use symbols and imagination like buses to carry them toward the goal.

Occultists not only participate in the world, but aim to build a ladder between the material world and the divine through their lives. This ladder of imagination enables people to journey to the throne of the divine being and then return the same way. The process enables the personality to be purified and, as a vehicle for the divine being, to express itself in matter. They can use their knowledge to manifest their experience on the material plane of existence.

Building in Mystical Experiences to Pathworkings

A pathworking can be adapted to make them more spiritual and less psychological or magical. The approach has to be less narrative and more feelings. Patience is required as a mystical experience cannot always be guaranteed and must be waited upon, and the person performing the pathworking has to be properly prepared.

The main focus of a mystical pathworking is a symbol of devotion. These are usually a token of faith from a religion, a symbol of a deity to whom one feels attached, either by birth or by conversion. This could be a crucifix or a cross if you are a Christian, a Talmud if you are Hebrew, a Tree of Life if you are a cabbalist, a statue or image if you are a neopagan, or anything that suggests a link between you and deity. In this book, which is multisecular, I have shied away from conventional forms of worship so that this information is accessible to all. To do this, I have adopted the powerful symbol of deity as being light or energy. This symbol is common to practically all religions.

The next thing involves some form of worship. Now I don't mean the mindless devotion where people prostrate themselves before something they perceive as much bigger than them and that needs appeasing. That approach only aims to create some kind of separation between deity and the person. If you think that deity is too big and powerful to enter into a personal relationship, then you will never believe that you can truly merge with that force. If we look at St. Teresa of Avila's description of a mystical experience as a marriage, then the first thing that needs to happen is some sort of friendship between you and your deity.

A pathworking can help this process by allowing a person to meet in his or her mind the divine being in the safe space of their imagination. A relationship can then develop as you start to see this deity appearing in your life. This relationship will be like any other: there will be moments when you disagree, agree, fall out, fall in, share highs and lows, etc. There is a certain naivety involved in this approach and, indeed, it is based on how a child sees deity. That is because in the initial stages of relating to deity, we are children who need a divine friend. There is nothing wrong in seeing deity this way.

Humor is very important. If you look at the truly great mystics, those that were not insane had a very good sense of humor; a mystical pathworking should allow this aspect of divinity to come through.

This phase of the relationship is often the most dangerous. It is where the ego and psychological weaknesses manifest to eclipse what would be a beautiful experience. The lower self will always try to shout down the voice of the divine with its own. Unfortunately, this is all too easy for it to do. We all want to think that the way we live our life is the divine's will, and if the lower self can put words into a deity's mouth to justify laziness, or even atrocities, then it will. The answer to this is to be careful and also know that the divine is not interested in controlling you. It is unlikely that it would have given you free will if it wanted to do that. So you will never be commanded to do anything by your deity. The divine wants to see the world through your eyes, your experiences, and your approaches with those things good, bad, or indifferent so that it leads to an understanding all on its own.

Moreover, the divine will not step away from the boundaries set by the religion through which it chooses to manifest to you. If you are a Christian and are using pathworking to deepen your mystical relationship with Christ, you are not going to find him telling you to steal or not love another. A Moslem or a Jew is not going to be told to eat pork or ignore the call to worship. In this way, it is possible to test some of the stranger things that your "deity" may say by comparing them with what is written in the Bible, the Koran, or even the legends of the gods themselves.

After a while, this human side of deity should be allowed to fall away, and as more of the deity's true nature is revealed, it becomes less anthropomorphized and more divine. Because the mind has been conditioned by repeated pathworking, it will connect this newer, more powerful version of deity as the friend with whom a relationship was forged. As the divine image separates from the human images, generally the worshipper goes with them. In fact, the changes are often so gradual that the worshipper does not notice.

The pathworking then is becoming something less subjective. Not only is the relationship "real" but the lines between the personality and the deity start to blur. Ultimately, this would lead to a total union, but even the short term can lead to a gradual awakening of the divine self.

Mystical pathworkings must always have this end in mind. Whereas a normal pathworking might lead to a realization about the nature of the universe, or an understanding about the self, a mystical pathworking always ends with some kind of union. A description of this union can be found in the German mystic Meister Eckhart's *Sermons and Treatises*.[6]

> You should love him as he is; a non-God, a non-spirit, a non-person, a non-image; rather as he is a sheer pure limpid one, detached from all duality. And in that one me may eternally sink from nothingness to nothingness.

Somehow a pathworking must lead to this almost Zen-like state where there is nothing, but everything. One would think it impossible to do this as words would instantly limit the vision. Where words limit, imagination provides the rainbow bridge that connects Earth to Heaven. If you have used just enough words that can point to the mystical experience without describing it, you have the essence of a good mystical pathworking.

What follows are a series of exercises and pathworkings that provide a mystical curriculum that will lead you over a period of months through several mystical experiences, perhaps ending up with some form of real awakening.

Preparation for Mystical Experience

Before you start, you should have visualization exercises that declare that a more mystical exercise has begun. It also works to balance the pathworker's aura so that more serious work can be done.

The preparation one most commonly used in the Western Mystery Tradition is the cabbalistic cross. Although this appears Christian, the symbolism is generic to most religions within the West.

The Cabbalistic Cross

The cabbalistic cross is a ritual visualization exercise that balances energy and seals the electromagnetic shell around the body, which is known as the aura. It places you under the protection of divine forces and, with regular use, strengthens the aura. The cabbalistic cross is performed before and after a pathworking to harmonize the energy that you have received in your meditation work. Like many magicians, I would perform the cabbalistic cross before I do any pathworking and afterward to help integrate the energies from the experience into my aura.

Cabbalistic Cross Exercise

Standing upright, close your eyes and visualize a bright, white ball of light above your head. This is the highest expression of the power of deity you are capable of conceiving at this time. Visualize this ball of light until you can almost feel the warmth on the top of your head. Visualize it beginning to spin.

Say the Hebrew word ATAH [Ah-tah], which means "thou art." Touch your forehead with the fingertips of your right hand and see a line of light from the white sphere travel down to where your fingers are touching your forehead.

Draw your fingers in a straight line down the center of your body and your breast. See the light follow your fingers and carry on down toward a white sphere, which is just below and encompassing your feet. As the light pours into this sphere, see it glow, brighten, and spin.

Say the Hebrew word MALKUTH [Mahl-kooth], which means "the Kingdom."

Tap your right shoulder and see a white sphere start to spin. Say the Hebrew words VE GEBRAH [Ve Ge-boor-ah], which mean "and the Power."

Draw another line of white across your body to your left shoulder and visualize another sphere of bright light starting to spin.

Say the Hebrew words VE GEDULAH [Ve Ge-doo-lah], which mean "and the Glory."

Now bring your hands together over your heart where the lines of light meet. Hold your hands as if you were praying.

Say the Hebrew words LEH OLAM [Lay Oh-lam], which mean "forever, amen."

See white light expand from your heart until your entire body is enclosed in a sphere of white light.

See yourself as a cross of light tipped with glowing spheres, and your aura filled completely with white light.

The Middle Pillar

The middle pillar is a key part of your preparation work and will have a noticeable effect on you within a few weeks. It opens energy centers, balances out the personality, and awakens a realization of the divine within. Although much of it starts as an imagination exercise, it is far more than that and is actually a form of practical magic. This is why the technique involves chanting a divine name to make it more powerful.

The exercise was developed into its current form by Israel Regardie from a complex Golden Dawn technique called "Building the Tree of Life in the Aura." It has echoes of Eastern tantric practice in that it involves a purification of the aura and the body by raising personal energy, or kundalini, to meet divine energy. By linking the two energy flows, it is possible to purify and revitalize the aura, raising it to a higher state.

As the energy flows through the body, it ejects coarser matter, refining the body so that it can handle more mystical experiences. It also sends a powerful message to the unconscious that it is in alignment with divine forces.

The middle pillar differs from Eastern practice in that it does not deal directly with energy centers (or chakras), but works on a level above them. This makes it safer for those who cannot practice under a trained guru because it does not allow different parts of the body to become overstimulated by the energies encountered.

Regardie considered the middle pillar exercise so important that he recommended any serious magical or mystical student to perform it twice a day at least. I agree. Anyone who does this exercise as much as this will truly transform his or her life extremely quickly.

Note: To vibrate the names given in the following exercise, take a deep breath, then push the sound to the roof of the mouth while contracting the throat. When say the word this way, you will feel vibrations deep within your throat and nose. The best place to experiment with this technique is in the bathroom where the acoustics will help you find the right pitch. Vibrating the words is somewhat loud, so it is best to practice when there is no one else at home.

Middle Pillar Exercise

Take a deep breath and visualize the white ball of light above your head. See it expand and begin to spin. Vibrate the divine name EHEIEH [Eh-hey-yay], which means "I am." Do this six times.

Imagine the light flowing down to a white ball of light at the nape of your neck. See it expand and begin to spin. Vibrate the divine name YHVH ELOHIM [Yod-hey-vav-hey El-oh-heem], which means "the Lord God." Do this six times.

Imagine the light flowing down to a white ball of light at heart. See it expand and begin to spin. Vibrate the divine name YHVH ELOAH VA-DAATH [Yod-hey-vav-hey El-oh-ah Ve-dah-arth], which means "the Lord God of Knowledge." Do this six times.

Imagine the light flowing down to a white ball of light at the groin. See it expand and begin to spin. Vibrate the divine name SHADDAI EL-CHAI [Sha-dye El-Chai], which means "Almighty living God." Do this six times.

Imagine the light flowing down to a white ball of light at the feet. See it expand and begin to spin. Vibrate the divine name ADONAI HA-ARETZ [Ah-doe-nye Ha-aretz], which means "the Lord of the Earth." Do this six times.

Allow the light to begin to encircle your aura. Begin on the left side, at about the same distance as your outstretched arm. Let it flow over your head to your right side, then under your feet to your left side. Continue to do this for a while.

When the light reaches the top of your head, change its direction to flow down your front to your feet, then under them.

Examples of Mystical Pathworkings

There are as many ways to approach the divine mystically as there are mystics. It would be impossible for any writer to give a definitive mystical pathworking that is guaranteed to resonate with the reader. Here are several pathworkings that have worked for me. As I have said earlier, I have attempted to keep these as free as possible from a link with any specific modern religion.

Lighting the Pharos Example

This pathworking was developed from an idea suggested at a workshop run by David Goddard that I attended in the mid 1990s. His idea was to take the person through the building of a lighthouse, or pharos, on the inner planes and then turn it over to others to use that light for their own purposes.[7] When it came to the lighting of the pharos flame, I experienced a beautiful white light with shafts of gold. This was a true mystical experience for me, and it occurred to me that if the symbol of the light house were adapted for pathworking, it could be used for personal mystical experiences. This version is a hard pathworking to get right and do not be surprised if it takes several attempts and you return exhausted.

Before you is a doorway with a blue curtain upon it. On the curtain, in silver, is the outline of a lighthouse or pharos. It looks like this:

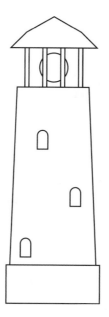

Figure 10: A Lighthouse

You concentrate on the doorway and the outline glows with power. The doorway becomes transparent and you step through into the silver mist of the astral realm.

After a while, the mist clears and you find yourself standing on a headland overlooking the sea. It is an overcast day and the sun is beginning to set.

In front of you the land falls away, and there are sharp jutting cliffs with dark rocks at the foot of them. The waves crash against the rocks in an ever-rolling din.

To your right, there is an ancient pharos standing tall against the twilight.

Its lamp is not yet lit.

You walk over to the huge double doors of the pharos. In your hand is a key. You don't know where you got it from, but somehow you realize that this pharos is yours and you are responsible for it.

You enter the pharos and find, much to your surprise, that you have not walked into a functional lighthouse but something that looks more like a temple.

All around you are intricate mosaics depicting aspects of creation, animals, people, and places. When you look closer, the scenes are all from parts of your life, molded in semiprecious stones and crystals.

On the ceiling, there is painted a night's sky with a zodiac border. Planets have been laid out in the shape of your astrological chart. In the center of the room is a spiral staircase.

This room represents your material world. The material world is not the light. You seek the light and that is on the upper levels.

You start to climb the staircase. You are aware that as you do so, part of you is being left behind: your family, your job, and the life that is around you. You have to find the light of the pharos.

You reach the next floor. It is filled with a silver astral mist. Around the walls are seven statues of angels, each of them representing a planetary force. There is angel of the sun, Mercury, Mars, Venus, Jupiter,

Saturn, and the moon. The statues look very lifelike, and the energy around their hearts beats with a special kind of inner light.

They are very powerful, but their light is not enough for you. You seek the main light of the pharos.

You continue slowly up the stairway again. It is an odd feeling as you climb past this room. You are aware that you are slowly allowing your attachment to your emotional and intellectual existence to slip away as you climb each step. You cannot think or even feel, you just are.

The next room is full of light—a rainbow of colors and energies. In the midst of these you can make out four bright lights. These are the very energies that the universe, thought, and emotion are made from. They are fire, water, air, and earth, but these are not just in a physical sense but in a deep and symbolic way.

The light of these room is not bright enough, and somehow even the hint of matter and thought seem hollow in comparison to the bright light that you know must be at the top of the pharos.

You keep climbing. You are aware that there is nothing really left of you other than an infinity of thought: not intellectual, or emotional, or controlled thought, but pure thought. You feel timeless and free.

You come out on top of the pharos into absolute darkness. Cold winds whip around you. There is driving rain. Below you, the sea is whipped to a frenzy. At the top of the pharos there is only an empty golden bowl and no light.

After all you have rejected, how can it be so lightless here? You feel crushed.

Lightning carves the sky. The storm is getting worse. It seems there is nothing you can do. You are cold and alone and have rejected everything that could have given you balance.

In a moment, you realize that in the midst of darkness there must be light, that the darkness is but an expression of the light you have been seeking, that even the storm is but an expression of light. Suddenly, you are at home in the darkness, but still hungry for the dawn. In your heart there is a call for the light, which you shout at the top of your lungs.

"FIAT LUX, FIAT LUX, FIAT LUX!"

Suddenly bursting on the golden dish is a bright diamond light. The light is not white but something more. It is everything born of nothing. It is outside you and within you. It just is. It lights up the storm.

It burns you.

It burns away the last of all feelings of separateness.

You are the light and it is you.

You are timeless.

Limitless.

ONE.

(Very long pause)

Slowly, the feeling of separateness grows again, and you find yourself looking into the diamond light. The storm is stilled.

Beside you is an unlit golden lamp.

You take the lamp and light it from the pharos flame.

You walk to the staircase and back down to the next level taking the lamp with you.

The four bright lights of the elements glow with power as you enter, singing a beautiful devotion to the light you carry. They start to move, and you are aware that they are moving in a new life pattern to the one you had before this vision of the pharos light.

You re-enter the next level, and you find the statues of the angels moving to form different patterns. You feel they have been awakened strongly by the sight of your lantern. You descend further into the final level.

To your surprise, all the crystals and semiprecious stones that depict your life glow with the light of the lantern. Every picture seems centered on the light, vibrant and living. You put your lantern down and marvel at the beauty of the divine light reflected in all you do.

Then, leaving your pharos and knowing that you will remember all that you have seen, even if you can't express it, you walk toward the doorway.

Before stepping into this time and space, you turn to see the pharos lighting up the whole night's sky.

You step through the doorway and become aware of this time and this reality.

The Trials of Maat Example: Part One

This pathworking has a Golden Dawn flavor and works with the symbolism used in that magical order. Its aim is to try the candidate so that he or she will be free from the bounds of the earthly realm and may become truly connected with his or her Higher Self. It uses the symbolism of the judgment hall of Maat that we first saw in chapter 4. Only here, the symbols are tuned in a slightly different way for a different end.

Unlike the pharos pathworking, this particular one aims at a purification of the soul, the turning away from the lower self and the integration of the High Self within the personality. This is a mystical experience for the Higher Self, which is said to be a reflection of the unity that is the Divine Mind.

This pathworking is in two parts. This is to allow its power to filter into a person's life. Neither are to be undertaken lightly, because they are turning the forces of cosmic justice upon you. While this is unlikely to do any long-term harm, the pathworkings are likely to force a balance in your life very quickly.

Imagine a huge doorway before you. On the lintel is a sun disk with rainbow wings. On the door is a painting of a huge set of scales. Focus your attention on the scales until they glow with power.

Say to yourself, "I, (state your name), proclaim myself to be a humble seeker after the Light of Wisdom and the Splendor of the Divine. I invite the beings behind the creation of the universe to test my resolve and enable me to find the Divine Light."

There is a voice from behind the door. "Why do you seek this?"

What is your reply?

The door opens and standing before you is a being with a jackal head wearing a nemyss of white and black stripes. He has in his left hand a caduceus, and in his right hand a lantern with a red flame. This is Anubis.

He says, "All beings who wish to partake of the Divine Light must be tested. Are you willing?"

If you agree, then the jackal-headed god will allow you to enter the gate. He says, "Enter thou then the halls of justice, the place of truth, the judgment hall of Maat."

You find yourself in a vast Egyptian temple. It is the color of flame.

Arranged in a semicircle before you are figures seated on thrones cut from red sandstone. They are dressed alike in kilts and nemyss of black and yellow. Some are human, but others are animals. Each wears a necklace in the shape of a flying hawk and carries a flail in the left hand. These are the forty-two assessors, the force of cosmic justice that judges even the gods.

In the center of the room is a black altar, and behind that are two pillars: one white and one black. In front of the pillars are a giant pair of scales.

Between the pillars is a woman wearing a nemyss striped black and white. Her linen gown is white and she holds a miter-headed wand. This is Maat.

Behind her on a throne is a human with a nemyss of striped white and yellow. He is wearing a white crown and is holding a white crowned scepter. This is Osiris.

Looking to your right, you see another jackal-headed god in a black and white kilt. He has a red sword in his hand.

Maat looks at you with eyes that pierce your very soul and says, "Inheritor of a dying world, arise and enter the darkness."

Anubis turns to you and says, "Unpurified and unconsecrated, you can go no further."

Two goddesses approach you. One carries a torch and the other a silver chalice. The one with the torch passes the flame through you. You feel no pain, just a feeling that something dross has been removed from you. Then the other goddess pours the water over you. You don't feel wet, simply cleaner.

Osiris says, "Inheritor of a dying world, thou hast sought admission to the mysteries of Light. But before you may enter into one of its lamps, the assessors who administer cosmic justice must test you. These tests are subtle. Are you willing to face them?"

What is your reply? Remember you are still allowed to leave.

Osiris says, "Very well. I shall give you a symbol that shall carry you through this test. Meditate on it often and uncover its meanings."

What is this symbol?

Maat comes from behind the scales.

She says, "You are a being of light, incarnate within a personality. Call upon your Higher Self in times of stress. Are you now prepared to be tested?"

What is your final reply?

Maat says, "Thrice (he or she) has been asked and thrice (he or she) has accepted."

Anubis stands to your left hand, Maat to your right. Osiris points his wand at you and you find yourself in a triangle of force.

The assessors outstretch their arms, pointing their fingers toward the scales. The scales begin to glow with power.

Maat says to you, "You must answer the following questions truthfully, to see if you are worthy of the Light that you seek. All that falls short of the Glory of Truth shall be bought into balance over time. Do you understand?"

Then begins the questioning. Each assessor stands and asks a question, which you must answer either yes or no. Each question is meant to be interpreted in its widest possible sense. Take your time in answering each one.

Have you committed sin?

Have you committed robbery with violence?

Have you stolen?

Have you killed?

Have you stolen food?

Have you taken things that were meant to be offerings for deity?

Have you stolen the property of deity for your own purpose?

Have you lied?

Have you wasted resources?

Have you cursed someone?

Have you wasted your sexuality?

Have you made people unhappy?

Have you worked to destroy your own spirit?

Have you attacked anyone?

Have you deceived?

Have you tried to take another's life work?

Have you been an eavesdropper?

Have you slandered a person?

Have you been angry without just cause?

Have you corrupted someone sexually for your own ends?

Have you tried to destroy another person's love?

Have you respected your body?

Have you terrorized someone?

Have you broken the laws of society?

Have you been an angry person?

Have you ignored the truth?

Have you blasphemed?

Have you lived a life of violence?

Have you stirred up strife?

Have you acted with undue haste?

Have you pried into another's life?

Have you spoken too much?

Have you wronged anyone or done evil?

Have you performed black magic?

Have you prevented people from finding the divine in their life?

Have you raised your voice?

Have you cursed the divine?

Have you acted with arrogance?

Have you sought to undermine religion?

Have you refused to honor the dead?

Have you stolen from the innocent or not respected the gods of
your land?

Have you persecuted those who have a different religion?

The assessors and gods return to their seats.

Maat says, "All things of which you have spoken shall be forgiven if
they are allowed to be corrected on my scales. Unbalanced power is the
ebbing away of life. Unbalanced mercy is weakness and fading away of

the will. Unbalanced severity is cruelty and barrenness of mind. Therefore, my judgment shall be that you shall become balanced."

She walks over to you and leans into your heart to take the energy of your soul, which manifests as a pink ball of light.

She places your soul upon the left side of the scales and takes the red feather of truth from her head and places on the right side. The scales start to dip, but instead she moves them with her hands so that the scales become in perfect balance.

She takes your soul, places it back into your heart, and proclaims, "In balance the Higher Self may come to thee. You are a being of light, incarnate within a personality——call upon your Higher Self in times of stress."

Osiris says, "Inheritor of a dying world, return to this place in a month to face our judgment."

Anubis returns you to the pylon gate, and you return to this place and this time.

The Trials of Maat Example: Part Two

Perform the cabalistic cross and middle pillar exercises. Relax, and get into the deepest stage of relaxation possible. Visualize before you a gateway of pink sandstone. On its lintel is a winged sun disk, and it has a curtain of red silk instead of a door. On the silk curtain is an image of pair of golden scales.

Speak the following to the door, "I, (state your name), proclaim myself to be a humble seeker after the Light of Wisdom and the Splendor of the Divine. At the request of Maat I return to receive judgment at the halls of Maat for reward or punishment."

Nothing happens.

After a while, you grow impatient and part the curtain yourself.

Inside, the judgment hall of Maat is empty and dark. The thrones are bare, and all that you recognize is the scales of Maat, which seem unbalanced. You walk toward them.

There is a crash of thunder.

You hear a howl of some unearthly creature behind you.

You remember what happens to people who fail the judgment of Maat . . . their hearts are fed to the crocodile-headed god Ammut. Your heart races, and you fear for the first time that you may have actually failed the test of the gods and now must face divine judgment.

There is a flash of lightning, and to your left you briefly see the out-line of a beast that has the head of a crocodile and the tail of serpent.

It is everything you fear.

You recoil into the scales. You call for Anubis, or Maat, or indeed anyone, but you are alone with this beast.

There is a flash of lightning, and you again see the beast this time walking toward you.

"Inheritor of a dying world, doomed to death and suffering, why do you tarry here?" the beast says.

The beast's form changes into a human. Who is it?

It continues, "Return to thine own realm to live and die in my clutches."

It walks toward you, and its hands become claws.

You turn and run toward the east of the temple.

Each step becomes harder to take. It is as if you are running in slow motion. Ammut is walking quickly toward you.

You can almost smell his breath.

And you are alone.

Then you remember the words of Maat: "You are a being of light, incarnate within a personality——call upon your Higher Self in times of stress."

You focus on your heart center and see it as a closed rose.

"Divine spark, reveal thyself," you say.

The rose in your heart opens to a blinding white light.

From the center of the white light comes a golden boy sitting on a lotus. He is wearing a crown, and has his index finger from his left hand touching his lips. This is Harparkrat.

Deep within yourself, you realize that you and this god are one. This divine spark is born of the infinite.

Time stops.

There is just you and Harparkrat.

"I am thee and thou art me," he says. "Purified and consecrated by flame, water, judgment, and life in the material world, we are partakers of the Light Divine. Let us join and be one and never forget this truth."

He merges into you.

What do you feel?

(Long pause)

You turn to face the frozen face of Ammut. You are energized by the combined power of you and your Higher Self. Time begins again.

Ammut flees.

You hear the most beautiful music.

Proceeding into the temple come the gods, closely followed by the initiates from countless traditions, each wearing the different robes of their orders.

They are all singing a welcome into the mysteries for a human who has met (his or her) own shadow and realized (his or her) divine nature enough to send evil fleeing.

You turn to see Osiris again on his throne.

"Creature of Earth. You have met and passed our test, although the fruits of this combat will continue for some time to come."

He hands you a golden box. You open it.

What is the gift of the gods?

The gods and initiates of the mysteries raise their arms in a salute of acknowledgement.

Anubis returns you to the gate.

He says, "May you find the truth you are seeking."

You say farewell, step through the gate, and return to this time and this place.

Ascending to the Throne of the Divine Example

This pathworking is one that I wrote for a reasonably experienced group. It does require abilities that will be initially beyond the beginner's scope, however, the more you practice, the easier it will become. You will also experience an ever-increasing depth with the pathworking until the experience becomes incredibly special.

This pathworking uses a similar technique to that is called "Rising on the Planes" that was developed by the Esoteric Order of the Golden Dawn.

The process used is similar to the one you will undergo after you die, where you ascend through the levels of creation, casting off those elements of you that are transitory and not your true spiritual self.

While the pathworking flippantly describes the casting off of the different aspects of personality, this is harder than it seems and can really only be done at death! Each time you practice this pathworking you can push away more ephemeral elements. The extent to which you can do it will mark your success at this pathworking.

It is best to make sure you do the pathworking just before bed or when you have not much else to do afterward, as it will take a while for the various parts of yourself to catch up afterward. This request for a break afterward needs to be heeded, in order to enhance the experience. There are some who say the pathworker should return the way he or she entered, gradually taking on the various emotional and intellectual bodies that were shed along the way. However, these bodies will align themselves fairly quickly after the pathworking is complete. The aim of this pathworking is to not only give the pathworker a profound mystical union with the divine, but also to give the person the feeling of what it is like to be a divine being incarnate in matter. The union will also give the pathworker a break from his or her complexes, roving thoughts, and emotions for a while, which can be a welcome respite!

Relax deeply until you cannot feel your body any more. In your mind's eye, feel yourself become lighter. Ascend your consciousness until it is hovering above your body. It feels wonderfully light to be free of your body.

You feel yourself rising through the air and into the sky. Soon you are aware that this sky is the astral level. You are surrounded by sparkly mist. There are images in the mist, and part of you wants to explore, but you feel you must press on further upward.

After a while, your upward journey is halted. It feels like you reached a barrier. You find it hard to go on, and then a quiet voice inside you says, "Your intellect is not needed here. Let it go." You push away your intellectual understanding of what is going on, taking it off like a cloak. From now on what you see will not or cannot be intellectually understood.

See for a moment what it is like to sense things just with feeling, not understanding them, but as they just are.

You feel lighter again, and start to ascend further.

Ahead of you is a light, like a beautiful star. With your emotional vision you know it is that which you have been looking for. It is your missing part, your divine self.

As you get closer, you start to see that space is bending around the light, pushing it backward so that is at right angles to reality and appears to be at the end of a tunnel. The tunnel walls are made up of swirling energy of color like a rainbow.

You ascend toward the tunnel, seeking to enter it. The walls of the tunnel are not just energy: they are beings. They are singing the most beautiful music. You feel all the emotion and joy within the song.

You can go no further. You are standing, beholding this vision of the light, yet there is something standing in your way.

"Your emotions stand in your way. You must let them go too," says the voice again, which is louder.

You shed your emotions like a cloak. All that you have ever felt is no longer with you. All that remains is a seed of your own personality, a center of consciousness that is timeless.

Take a moment to experience what this is like with spiritual vision. The tunnel is so much more alive now, and the song you hear can now be felt with every essence of your being. Symbols whirl in the rainbow-colored vortex.

In front of you, the light is diamond, pure, not white but clear.

You move toward the light through the tunnel. As you get closer, the light burns and yet attracts you at the same time. Suddenly, you feel you can get no closer to the heart of the light and never leave the tunnel. Although the tunnel is beautiful, it is not as lovely as the light you see before you. You feel disheartened; it is as if there were an abyss of darkness between you and the light you seek.

Then the voice says, "There is no difference between you and the light. The self that watches is the same as the light at tunnel's end."

Then you realize you must shed that concept of who you are. You are not an incarnate being, but you and the light are one.

The moment this happens, you step into the timeless and limitless light. You dissolve into it like sugar into water. You become the light.

Timeless.

(Long pause)

After a while, you feel that you want to know something, something unique about yourself. You imagine the universe.

You imagine the world with a life on it.

You imagine a person in that world.

You imagine that person's life up to this point.

Then you shift a part of yourself into that person.

Open your eyes.

You are the rider in a chariot.

You are an infinite divine being expressing itself in a personality.

See the light around you with your divine eyes.

See your life with the new vision.

Know that this is how you truly are.

When you are ready, allow yourself to return to this time and place. Have a drink or something to eat, and write down what you have experienced.

CHAPTER SEVEN

Gates to the Inner Kingdoms

Throughout this book I have referred to the use of door as methods of entering your Inner Kingdom or the astral plane. So far a door's use has been as part of a fairly controlled experiment, with a particular doorway important to the flavor of the pathworking. In this chapter, instead of a door we will look at the different types of gates, where the territory that lies behind them is uncertain.

The Western Mystery Tradition uses many different types of gates, with the aim of experiencing different aspects of reality. Each gate has a symbol upon it, and what lies beyond the gate always relates to an understanding of the symbol.

Generally, these gates are used to access spiritual, emotional, or spiritual principles. Such principles might be an abstract idea like love, or a power that is experienced within a symbolic landscape. Someone entering a gate of Mars, for example, could find themselves visiting the scene of a battle or work at a blacksmith's forge. These principles have definite locations, flora, and fauna.

It is tempting to think of these as dream worlds. However, as we saw earlier, such landscapes have both a subjective and objective reality. Remember these worlds are built on the principle of Plato's world of ideas. What happens in these worlds may have an impact on the reality below or reflect it in symbolic form.

Visiting such worlds through gates shows you: (1) what you think of the principle, and (2) how it really is. Some of these symbols are extremely abstract, others are fairly obvious, however, all symbols need to be analyzed after the pathworking is completed

These gates are like one depicted in the science-fiction movie *Stargate,* in that the people making their first journey have no real idea where they are going or what they will see on the other side. A person should pass though the gate with an open mind after reflecting upon the symbol, and gaze upon the landscape as if he or she was a tourist. No one has described beforehand what he or she might see; the "tourist" is just entering into it and describing what is on the other side of the gate for himself or herself. This is clairvoyant vision, and does not need for the person to be particularly "psychic" to achieve results.

This freeform clairvoyance make such journeys less productive than guided meditations because the beings on the other sides of these gates often have little understanding or interest in humanity. This does not necessarily mean they are "aliens" in the *The X-Files* or *Close Encounters of the Third Kind* sense. Normally, these are creatures who are associated with a particular force, or the spiritual building blocks of the universe (elementals), and would pay scant attention to outsiders.

In dealing with such creatures, it is important to remember that if they notice you at all, they are unlikely to want to do your bidding or give you much notice. Some entities lack the ability to communicate at all. I remember one memorable working where I spent ages struggling to communicate with something that looked like a walking cactus, only to be told later that these "cacti" had the same function as sheep on that level.

Sometimes, it is possible to call upon a being to help you understand the level you are visiting. These guides will prove extremely helpful if they show up, and can be trusted.

Generally, you would ask for help in the name of the divine being (or beings) that applies to that level. If a guide shows up, then it must promise to help and protect you in the name of the deity of that level. For example, here is an example of a journey I had to the elemental plane of earth.

After stepping through the earth gate I found myself in a red cave, lit by glow worms. There were three stalactites, but there was nothing else around. I called for a guide in the name of Adonai Ha Aretz. Nothing happened. I tried again. This time I noticed a gnome leaning on a shovel. I asked him what he was, but he appeared disinterested. I asked if he will help me in the name of Adonai Ha Aretz. The gnome turned and looked at me with fear. "That name is not for the likes of me, for it burns like molten fire in my blood."

I sat and waited, and still nothing. I resolved to chant the name Adonai Ha Aretz until something happened.

After a while, one of the stalactites said to me, "Who is it that calls the Name of the Lord of Earth?" I gave my name and asked the stalactite if he would be my guide in the name of Adonai Ha Aretz. The stalactite said he will do so to the best of his ability. "However," he added, "you should be aware that I am unable to move from this spot!"

I asked my guide some questions about itself and the gnome. The stalactite told me that he is a being that is slowly growing from the top of cave roof to the floor of the cave. After a while he would grow to reach the cave roof again. Then he would be a pillar for the cave and help support the roof.

The gnomes were earth elementals who were responsible for placing jewels in the earth. "Without these jewels, the earth would grow sick and die," said the stalactite. There was a pause as I wondered out loud how I could use this information. The stalactite said that I should see this scene as if it were an allegory. In this comparision, the earth is made up of congealed living energy that flows down from heaven. The energy grows in power until it has evolved to the point where it touches heaven again. Once it has achieved that, matter will become a support for the rest of creation. This is an extremely slow process, but it means that even stones and rocks are evolving.

Technique for Entering a Gate

This technique is taken from a Golden Dawn paper titled "Attaining to Spirit Vision."

1. Allow for an hour or longer of meditation completely free from interruption.

2. Relax.

3. Stand and perform the cabbalistic cross exercise (see last chapter). (The Golden Dawn would also have you say a prayer to the deity associated with the gate you are entering.)

4. Place before you the symbol that you will want to see on the gate. Gaze at the symbol until you see into it.

5. You should then deeply sink into the abstract idea of the symbol. Consider all its meanings.

6. Shut your eyes and visualize the symbol on a gate in front of you.

7. Step through the gate.

"The vision may begin by the concentration passing into a state of reverie; or with a distinct sense of change, something allied in sensation to a faint, with a feeling urging you to resist, but if you are highly inspired, fear not, do not resist, let yourself go; and then the vision will pass over you." [1]

Upon completion of the pathworking, it is important to return through the same gate. When you are approaching the gate from the inner plane side, the symbol will be there in clear detail on the gate but will be reversed, as if the gate and symbol were viewed from behind.

It is important to leave the same way you came in for several reasons. This helps the process of integration to spend some time journeying back, and allows the various aspects of the self to focus itself back on the physical body. More importantly, it trains the pathworker to return to his or her body through the same gate taken when the pathworking is finished. If you start to make the same journey in your sleep, or as part of an astral journey, where conscious control is harder, if you habitually return by the same gate you entered, it will be easier to unconsciously come back through the gate you started at.

If for some reason it is too difficult to return (for example, you might have wandered a long way from the gate), you can call the gate to you by asking for it to appear in the name of the deity (or deities) of that level and visualizing the symbol and gate appearing before you in detail, but only reversed.

It is important to remember that although some of these gates may appear to mean the same thing, they will all lead to different places and different experiences. Sometimes you will enter the same gate and end up in a different place because your mindset will have changed from the last journey.

Tattvic Gates

Tattvas were one of the few concepts from the East that entered the Western Magical Tradition at the end of the nineteenth century. Brought over by the Theosophists, one book in particular, *Nature's Finer Forces* by Rama Prasad, was a great influence on the magicians of the Golden Dawn. Tattvas are a series of symbols that represent the four elements (earth, fire, water, air) and a fifth, spirit.

The idea behind the tattvas are that there are unseen tides in the universe that are influenced by the elements. The tides of tattvas flow in an unseen medium known as *prana,* or etheric matter, which surround the sun and moves the Earth and other planets.

The element of *akasha* (spirit) is strongest at sunrise, then slowly changes to the element of *vayu* (air). This in it turn becomes *tejas* (fire), and then to *apas* (water), and finally merging into *prithivi* (earth), and the cycle begins again.

According to one Golden Dawn magician, John Brodie Innes, the tattva vayu promotes restlessness; tejas produces anger; apas encourages receptivity and contentment; and prithivi produces indifference. "You get mental activity from Vayu and mental fire and genius, invention from Tejas. You get receptivity and plastic turn of mind from Apas. You get firm and steadfast mentality and admirably sane and founding upon a rock from Prithivi. And so you may trace the mental condition of every human being and you may know precisely what tattvas have operated to produce that particular mind."[2]

As each tide moves on the Earth, they influence people (and even objects). If two people were feeling angry at each other, the appearance of the tejas current at that time might move them to violence. People have tattvic tides of their own, which are influenced by these forces and sometimes counteract the Earth's tidal flows.

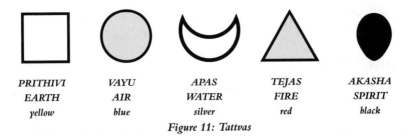

PRITHIVI	VAYU	APAS	TEJAS	AKASHA
EARTH	AIR	WATER	FIRE	SPIRIT
yellow	*blue*	*silver*	*red*	*black*

Figure 11: Tattvas

These tattvic symbols may be combined (for example, the red triangle of tejas may be placed in the center of the yellow square of prithivi) to give subtle elemental combinations that show, in this example, the fire in the heart of the earth.

The tattvas symbols are painted on a piece of black cardstock in their appropriate colors. The symbols are to be stared at for a few moments, then visualized as being placed on a gateway.

The cabbalistic names for each of these tattvas are Eheieh for spirit, El for water, Elohem Gibor for fire, Shaddai El Chai for water, and Adonai Malek for Earth.

Elemental Gates

These are a simpler version of the tattvas. Using these elemental symbols, again painted on a black card, give a more general overview of the elemental nature of the universe. There are five cards: fire, water, air, earth, and spirit. These cards can be combined in much the same way as tattvas by placing two cards in your hand and visualizing them both on the gate that you formulate in your mind's eye.

Fire △

Water ▽

Air ◬

Earth ▼

Hebrew Letters

There is a cabbalistic tradition that God created the universe using the Hebrew letters. It follows that using these letters as gates will unlock a considerable amount of information about how the universe works.

Each Hebrew letter has a number and a meaning, and these can reveal much about the sort of life one might encounter beyond the gate. The letter Aleph is attributed to the number 1 and means "Ox"; therefore one might expect to see an ox at some point of the pathworking.

In the Western Mystery Tradition, each path on the Tree of Life has a Hebrew letter allocated to it. Since these paths show the mixing of energies between the spheres on the Tree of Life, it gives an idea of the sort of energy one is likely to encounter beyond the gate. The letter Tau connects Malkuth with Yesod. This would mean a connection between the earth energies of Malkuth and the lunar energies of Yesod.

Not only does a pathworking give an understanding of each Hebrew letter, it also gives a deeper understanding of the names of power that are made up by those letters. The letters themselves are names of power and high-level angelic forces. Therefore, when doing a pathworking and you need to call upon a name of power, you should use the name of the letter.

The letters should be written in black lettering on a white card.

Name	Hebrew Letter	Meaning	Numeric value
Aleph	א	Ox	1
Beth	ב	House	2
Gimel	ג	Camel	3
Daleth	ד	Door	4
He	ה	Window	5
Vau	ו	Nail	6
Zayin	ז	Sword	7
Cheth	ח	Boundary	8
Teth	ט	Snake	9
Yod	י	Hand	10
Kaph	כ	Fist	20
Lamed	ל	Ox Goad	30
Mem	מ	Water	40
Nun	נ	Fish	50
Samekh	ס	Prop	60
Ayin	ע	Eye	70
Pe	פ	Mouth	80
Tzaddi	צ	Fish Hook	90
Qoph	ק	Back of the Head	100
Resh	ר	Face	200
Shin	ש	Tooth	300
Tau	ת	Cross	400

Figure 12: Images and Numbers Associated with Hebrew Letters

Planetary and Zodiacal Symbols

Although planetary and zodiacal symbols have become commonplace in modern astrology, their use as elemental gateways has rarely been examined. In fact, each symbol provides direct access to that planetary or zodiacal state of consciousness, and using them as gates can enhance your knowledge of their meanings.

This knowledge of planetary and zodiacal symbols proves valuable for astrologers seeking to deepen their knowledge of these planetary energies for chart interpretation. It also enables a deeper understanding of the various planetary and zodiacal influences in your own chart.

It is extremely useful for magicians to know in advance what the energy they are trying to use in a ritual will feel like. If you are doing a working that uses the planetary energy of Mars, for example, you will know that you have pulled through enough energy when the room feels like a Mars pathworking performed prior. You will also have a clearer idea of how the particular energy works on you.

Remember that the effect of a pathworking is often to bore holes through the consciousness and allow better access to that energy. Working with the planetary and zodiacal forces will intensify and enable those forces to be expressed on the material levels much better.

Unlike the elemental gates, planetary and zodiacal symbols are best painted on a round disk the size of a dinner plate using a technique called "flashing colors." The disk should be painted in the appropriate planetary color with the planetary symbol painted in its given color. The resulting optical illusion gives the impression that the symbol is vibrating or flashing.

Planetary Colors

Planet	Background	Gate Symbol	Symbol Color
Saturn	Black	♄	White
Jupiter	Blue	♃	Orange
Mars	Scarlet	♂	Green
Venus	Emerald	♀	Scarlet
Sun	Gold	☉	Purple
Moon	Violet	☽	Yellow

Zodiacal Colors

Zodiacal	Background	Gate Symbol	Approximate Flashing Color of Symbol
Leo	Deep Purple	♌	Yellow
Aries	Red	♈	Green
Sagittarius	Yellow	♐	Purple
Taurus	Deep Indigo	♉	Yellow
Capricorn	Black	♑	White
Virgo	Gray	♍	White or Black
Aquarius	Sky Blue	♒	Orange
Gemini	Pale Mauve	♊	Yellow
Libra	Blue	♎	Orange
Scorpio	Brown	♏	Blue Green
Pisces	Buff	♓	Blue Green
Cancer	Maroon	♋	Blue Green

The effect of using flashing colors as elemental gates is tremendous. This is partly because the adepts of the Golden Dawn place these symbols in their flashing colors on devices called flashing tablets, which attract blind planetary force for use in talisman making, ritual, or alchemy.[3] Using them as planetary or zodiacal gates means that the pathworker is exposed to the planetary energy before he or she enters the gate. This also means that the pathworker would experience the energy at a much deeper level because his or her inner vision is properly attuned to the planetary energies.

Tarot Cards

Tarot cards are the perfect magical gates to interior realities. The more esoteric Hermetic packs, like those of the Builders of the Adytum, Chic and Tabatha Cicero's *Golden Dawn Magical Tarot,* or Aleister Crowley's *Thoth* pack, are designed with this purpose in mind.

Not only do they contain symbols of inner realities that effectively stir the mind, they also feature Hebrew letters, colors, planetary, and elemental and cabbalistic attributions that could take a lifetime of study.

The esoteric group Builders of the Adytum are fond of saying that if you were washed up on a desert island with nothing but a tarot deck, you could unlock the secrets of all esoteric wisdom. There is some truth to this, and if you used the tarot cards as gates, you really would gain a considerable amount of esoteric knowledge.

The major arcana of the tarot deck is closely linked, by modern occultists, to the paths on the Tree of Life, and the minor arcana with the spheres (the Aces represent Kether, the Twos Chokmah, the Threes Binah, etc.). This means that the tarot can be used to unlock the secrets of the Christian Cabbalah, with each tarot card leading you to a mystical experience of the associated path. Dolores Ashcroft-Nowicki wrote a modern occult classic called *Shining Paths,* which gives pathworkings on the Tree of Life using tarot cards.

On a more mundane level, using the cards as gates considerably enhances your ability to understand the cards' meanings in divination. Once you have visited them all, turning over a card is like opening a photo album to a place that you have visited. When you apply what the querent is asking in relation to that experience, you will be able to give the querent a much deeper answer.

One of the Builders of the Adytum's magical techniques suggests that you become the central character in the tarot card. This gives you a deeper sense of the energy of the card and the characters within.

Figure 13: The Magician Card from the **Golden Dawn Magical Tarot**

Magical and Alchemical Drawings

For a long time, mystical and magical information was portrayed in symbolic form in drawings. These were particularly common in alchemy, where the process of transmutation was shown in obtuse symbolic language and pictures. Many of the keys to this language have been lost to modern minds, however, by using these drawings as gates we can unlock these particular mysteries. When using alchemical drawings it is important to realize that the illustrators were not simply showing chemical reactions, but rather a spiritual process that led to a total transmutation. The work represented in these drawings and their equally obscure writings could not only be enacted in a test tube but also in the magical imagination. Such drawings show in symbolic form a snapshot of a spiritual state. If an alchemical drawing is placed on an elemental gate, it is possible to visit that state and experience what it is showing you. Drawings of alchemical processes can be found in the *Book of the Lambspring* (translation by Adam McLean) or *Splendour Solis.*

Alchemical drawings should be experienced in order for them to have the best effect. Don't start using the alchemical drawings unless you are serious and ready to face the consequences of the change they will bring. Alchemy is advanced work and potentially life-changing.

Images of a God and Goddess

This is especially effective for neopagans who want to have a deep contact with their particular deity. All that needs to be visualized on the gateway is an image of the god or goddess that you feel most closely reflects your understanding of the particular deity. Sometimes the symbol might be an image of a statue or a painting, other times it might be a symbol or icon representational of that god or goddess.[4]

CHAPTER EIGHT

Life is but a Dream

In all the pathworkings you have carried out so far, you should have been aware there is an essential "you" that has been participating in the exercises. It did not matter if you were approaching the throne of heaven or the deepest aspects of your darker side, there was always a "you" that was the observer.

Once the pathworking is over and you are awake within your physical body, the "you" is still there observing. It may have better tools to perceive the world around it (such as the five senses) than it might have in any pathworking, but it is still the same observer. This begs the question: is this material world any different from any of the other worlds that we may have visited?

Essentially, there is little difference other than the fact that for some reason the spirit of humanity seems particularly attached to the World of Material level. Humans have a material, physical body, which is designed to live in this world, and makes this level appear more real, but this physical body also binds us to this level's rules. These rules are expounded to us by modern science, which has been good at telling us how the World of Material works. While we dwell in our bodies, we have to maintain them with food and shelter: food is needed to sustain the body, shelter is needed to protect our body from the physical environment.

This material world contains so many elements similar to our dream or imaginative worlds, and when we start to see this world as just one of many that we live in, then it is possible to interpret life as if it were a dream.

Think of some event in your life and then describe it as if you were telling a friend about a weird dream you had. Here is a fictitious example from a female office worker:

"I am in work and I am bored. The work is below what I am qualified to do, and I am always trying to make it seem more important than it is. There is a problem with my boss. He always seems to be finding fault with everything I do and it makes me feel very depressed. He is also a sexist pig who has made passes at girls in the office, and he makes life difficult for those who don't play ball."

The crucial symbol here is the person's boss. The boss could be a symbol of the autocratic father figure who constantly belittled her when she was small. The fact that he also sexually harasses women in the workplace could be an indication that her father perceived women as sex objects. There are elements of sexual blackmail, which are a reflection of the way this woman unconsciously sees what she has to do to please men.

The other symbol is the work, which represents self-achievement and progression. In this woman's case, work indicates she lacks the confidence to face the world with all her abilities. Instead, she tries to make do with second-best. The fact that she is bored, resentful, and unhappy indicates that she is holding on to the status quo even though she knows her present position is hurting her.

So by putting the two symbols together, we are left with an interpretation that might look like this:

"This woman had an autocratic father who constantly belittled her. This belittling has damaged her self-confidence to the point that she is scared to be her true self. Her success, which should be working on her own direction in life, is being instead directed into appeasing her father."

The "dream" would be suggesting that changing her work would be the best thing for her, as it would take her from the clutches of the bad father figure. Her work should be something that she is qualified for and finds fulfilling.

Here is another example, this time from a male train passenger in Britain:

"I went to work today and the train broke down due to leaves on the railway track. The train driver apologized for 'any inconvenience that the delay might have caused,' but no one believed him. I was angry because it is bloody typical of the inefficiency of Britain's Public Transport system."

Here is an event, which could be a symbol for how the person's life's journey is frustratingly slow as life's direction is being thwarted by small things beyond our control. A key symbol in the above description was that the person felt angry. Another person might have felt bemused about how a big train could be stopped by something as silly as leaves on the line. Another might have found this situation a joke! But this person was "angry," and used words that were similar to a parent scolding a child. This is further emphasized by the comment about the apology not being accepted. In effect, this person wants to be angry about something, to tell someone off because life is not progressing the way how he would like. This is someone who blames things outside himself for the situations he is facing.

The more unusual some aspect of your life appears in such a "retelling," the more important it is as a symbol of the way your life is going. The above train example is not unusual to most people's lives, and therefore cannot be taken too far, but if the train was delayed because a lion had escaped from a theme park and was lying on the track, this lion would be a much more important symbol.

When the Dream Becomes a Nightmare

Major life crises, such as death, divorce, and job upheavals, are packed with the most important symbolism, which, if correctly interpreted, can often prevent suffering in the same way again.

The nightmare situations in our life are mostly of our own making: we pick the wrong partner, job, or lifestyle. We usually have symbolic warnings that something bad is going to happen, which we blissfully ignore, and then our world collapses. If we see these crises as we would in an Inner Kingdom, with the key players as symbols, then we start to understand the nature of the world we have created around us. Our lives become fairy stories in which we experience and learn.

For example, I talked to Jermima, a victim of a man who wants to control every aspect of her life, right down to the clothes she wears. A talented artist, Jermima finds her skills put on hold as the duties of looking after her boyfriend become the key focus. She never leaves the house because her boyfriend is always suspicious of her movements. When he is away on business, he calls Jermima every two hours to make sure she is still at home. This is similar to the story of Cinderella, where the beautiful heroine is forced to cook and clean for her ugly sisters despite her ability to catch the handsome prince.

Someone comes into Jermima's life and shows her that there is an alternative way for her. Not quite a fairy godmother, the person explains that she is in this situation because she does not want to realize her full potential out of fear that success will bring responsibilities far more important than getting a meal on her boyfriend's table.

She is enthused about the possibilities of a new life and decides to escape, and if she had left to start her new life at this point, then the fairy story would be over. But like many fairy stories, there is an evil wizard involved.

Jermima decides to flee the boyfriend, but being insecure and still too frightened to risk starting out life on her own, she looks for another man on upon whom to start her "new life." She finds someone who seems to fit the bill, but he is actually a carbon copy of her boyfriend, but only worse. He is married and stringing her along with empty promises of a "new life" with him. Since he does not really want to care for her, he advises her to live with her boyfriend, even though the man makes her unhappy, and she agrees.

Now Cinderella is under the spell of an evil magician, and still trapped in her hellish existence.

The universe never gives up in trying to move a person closer to his or her true destiny, and so enters the fairy godmother figure again, this time in the guise of a twist of fate. The boyfriend throws her out- after finding love letters from Jermima to her married lover. Jermima looks to the evil magician to take her in, but since he is married, he turns his back on her.

Jermima is now alone and facing her worst nightmare——that she will be left alone. I made the remark that her life was remarkably like a fairy story. "But where is the handsome prince?" she cried.

The handsome prince was something within her: her personal strength, self-control, and the ability to make decisions for herself. These qualities frightened her because they bought responsibility, and her need for them was still great so she looked for them in her partners to balance herself out. Her fear meant that when Jermima chose her men with those desired character traits, she only chose those with the unbalanced aspects of them.

"But I never picked these men," she said. "They picked me!"

This comment, which is really common in cases where people pick controlling or violent partners, assumes that the "victims" were coerced or "under some spell" when they entered into the relationship. It has been my view that people enter relationships to fulfill some psychological need, either good or bad. In Jermima's case, it was to look for the missing part of herself, which she did not want to spend the time acquiring the discipline or self-reliance to find.

By working with the men in her life as symbols of her own self, Jermima could try and find the qualities she needs to develop.

But what of the other nightmares we develop in our lives? A particular bugbear is illness, which seems to spontaneously appear, often in a very nasty way.

The psychologist Wilhelm Reich (1897–1957) worked with cancer patients in the 1940s, and he became convinced that a particular type of person was more susceptible to the illness. These were people who gave up, refused to fight the problems in their lives, and were content to be victims. Those who were more aggressive about life were less likely to have cancer, or if they had cancer, were better at fighting it off. Reich's observations were noted by the authors of *Getting Well Again*, Carl Simonton and Stephanie Matthews-Simonton, who in 1978 concluded that people predisposed to cancer often had poor self-image, had a tendency toward self-pity, and to hold in resentment, personalities that often became "victims."

While this defeatist attitude could be a factor in the development of cancer, there are others as well, and it is simplistic to say that because someone has cancer he or she does not affirm life or that he or she doesn't want to fight it. Terminal illness is sometimes the only way that a soul can leave the present incarnation when its time is up. With all the life's work achieved, the body has to die of something, and illness is a logical way.

But cancer, or any illness, is a symbol, and its nature is up to the individual to interpret. While for some it might be the all-encompassing final nail in the coffin that ends their miserable and repressed lives, for others it can be a call to arms. Many who do fight off cancer say that they tend to live for each second, and this could be the symbolic result they need to understand. Whatever illness you might face, it is important to see what it represents to your life. If approached with the same care and testing that is used for an Inner Kingdom being, then the specific symbol of illness can reveal much.

You will notice that unlike many New Age writers, I do not say that illness is all in the mind and that you can overcome it entirely by using mental techniques or dealing with psychological blockages. By the time an illness has manifested on the material level, it is often too late to stop its effects. The body is a creature of the material world, and as such responds quicker to physical things like antibiotics and surgeries than it would by the power of the mind alone.

Magical imagination techniques will dispense with the need for the illness to manifest, as you will start to see the illness' appearance in the imagination beforehand, and there you can deal with it long before it affects you physically. But it is silly to refuse medication for asthma simply because you know the asthama is caused by an emotional need for affection. If you can't breathe properly, take your inhaler; and as you start to understand your emotional needs, you will find you need to take it less often. This could be the reason why childhood asthama disappears as the sufferers become more independent from their parents or find the emotional support they need in a relationship.

Also, I would be a little careful about focusing on health or any other aspect of the physical world too much. By all means see health, and particularly symbolic illnesses, as something to be looked at, but be careful about allowing such items to become an obsession, as a resulting self-feeding complex can be created within your Inner Kingdom.

So what of the so-called "random unlucky event," the mugging, the plane crash, the tragedy of a pedestrian killed by a car? Most of these random events can be understood by interpreting them as symbols. If you are the victim, write down what happened and interpret the event as a dream. Like a dream, you will be surprised at little details that have no meaning except as symbols of something else. For example, when processing a street mugging, Jason commented on what struck him as odd was that he never saw his attacker. He was attacked from behind and did not remember losing consciousness, yet he found himself in confusion on the ground with his wallet apparently spirited away as if by an invisible force. "The first thing I thought of was that I must have tripped, yet my coat was ripped off my shoulders. Then came the realization of what happened followed by a profound sense of loss," Jason said afterward.

I asked him what that loss felt like, and he said suddenly that it reminded him of when his lucky blanket was taken away from him by his father, who thought he was too old for such things, and thrown it into the trash. Jason thought it odd that he should remember the event that had taken place some thirty years before. After a while, Jason realized that for him the robbery was a symbol that anything material could be taken away, and that security needed to be based on things that were less tangible.

The death of a friend or family member also has incredible symbolic meanings. While it does not mean that something in your life actually caused it. Rather, the event has happened at a time when it can have the most meaning for you. People learn a lot about themselves when faced with the enormity of death. Often their response is to question their own mortality and attempt to find more meaning in their lives. Sometimes the deaths of strangers become symbolic for a whole group of people. The death of Princess Diana in a car crash, for example, evoked a worldwide emotional response in many people. But what I found interesting at that time was that many people who rushed to place flowers or attended the funeral procession in London were not actually mourning the death of a beloved public figure. Many used her death as a symbol to remember members of their families or friends who had died in similar circumstances. Princess Diana was a symbol of their own loss, which they could re-examine and process.

Being a Symbol

If other people and circumstances are symbolic to you, it is fairly obvious that you can be a symbol to other people. To your family, you might be the "Black Sheep" or the "Wonder Child" in whom all their dreams are realized. At work, you might be the "Heartless Boss," the "Moaning Employee," or the "Hard Worker Who Lacks Recognition" symbol. You might find yourself being someone's father or mother figure and get a lot of surprising flak as a result. This can cause problems if the symbol does not suit you, for example, if your boss sees you as the "Wayward Progeny" and because of this is always telling you off, even though you are a model employee.

It is possible to change the symbol that people see you by. Politicians, press officers, and other masters of proganda work hard to archive this all the time. They will seek to only associate themselves with situations in which they appear in a positive light. To a greater or lesser degree they succeed when they become a symbol for something else. But beware, for it is easier to become a negative symbol than it is to be positive one.

The power of people as symbols, particularly public figures, can never be underestimated. Margaret Thatcher, who managed to cultivate herself as a symbol of "Iron Authority," hung on to power despite extreme unpopularity in some quarters. Others where afraid to challenge this image. But Thatcher made a huge mistake late in her rule when the British public saw her trying to usurp the symbols of royalty (for example, starting to speak like Queen Victoria with such memorable quotations as "We are now a Grandmother"). In doing so, her symbol changed from "Iron Authority" to "Royal Usurper," and her cowed cabinet found the courage to stand up to her by defending the "True Queen" symbol. Any hope Thatcher might ever be asked to lead the Conservative Party again were finally dashed when she cried as she left Number 10 after being sacked—her "Iron Authority" image upon which her power depended was duly shattered.

Most people do not have to deal with the collective belief patterns of an entire nation, but the same principles apply. If you want to appear in everyone's eyes as a symbol of efficiency, you can adopt all the trappings that make you appear efficient: the slick suit, the personal organizer, and the tidy desk. It does not matter that the drawers are stuffed full of rubbish; the desktop must be extremely organized.

Con artists are always the most convincing if they manage to incorporate the symbols of what they are trying to impersonate. At the time of this writing, a moderately successful con-trick, in which an e-mail is sent to a person asking for their bank account details, turned into a spectacularly successful one as the con artists directed potential victims to a website that looked like a leading South African bank's. The webpage was covered with symbols of authority and stability that were unfortunately were fakes. Victims were prepared to overlook the bizarre requests for cash because the symbols suggested they were dealing with a legitimate bank.

This example leads to an important point. Attempting to associate yourself with a certain symbol will only work so far unless there is a genuine change behind it. This is because as people start to associate you with the symbol you wish to create, they will expect you to be like it all the time. When you fail to respond in the way they think you should, you will fail to represent that for them. This is true of any politician who has attempted to cover their failings with spin doctoring. After a while, voters start to realize that the politician they put in office no longer represents their wishes, and look for a new leader.

If you decide that you are going to represent a particular symbol, you should work with it to allow it to slowly reform your behavior patterns. You can act this out in your Inner Kingdom so that the subtleties of the symbol are played out in your mind first. There, you can act out the new you in a fairly safe environment so that you see how your new symbol and resulting behavior interacts with others.

The Internet is an excellent way of forming a halfway house between your Inner Kingdom and the outside world. In an Internet chat room you can be anything you want to be without be questioned. For example, while recovering from a lack of self-confidence caused by his marriage break-up, David did not have the courage to ask anyone out for a date. Aware that he had to create a new image for himself, he created a online character called Wizard, whom was a supremely confident flirt. In the half-world of the Internet, David found he could be this person. Even though at times David felt that Wizard was too much, many found the character attractive. Soon, David had to play the role of Wizard at a "real" party and, much to his surprise, he found it easy——and he also found it easy to get dates. Later, he was able to integrate the desired aspects of the Wizard character so that David reflected more of who he wanted to be.

There are some who feel that tinkering with your personality in this way is wrong. They believe that a person should feel confident to be himself or herself, and not attempt to be someone they are not. I do not believe that the true self, which is trying to be reflected through the personality, is at all negative. When people want to be themselves, it is that Higher Self they want to be, not a little bag of neuroses. One of my clients, Joan, said she was shy, and for six months attempted to be self-assertive and yet hated it. "I am shy and I cannot be someone else," she said. Later, she described the feeling of being shy as negative and I asked her if she felt her Higher Self was a negative being. "No," she said. "My Higher Self always appears as a very powerful angel figure."

"So not particularly shy then?"

"No."

So when Joan said she was shy and could not be someone else, she did not mean her true self. She was living in her personality and believing it was her real self, rather than the somewhat broken vehicle of her Higher Self. When she realized that her Higher Self was not shy, she successfully started to work on building her self-confidence.

Inner and Outer Kingdoms

Earlier I mentioned the case of a woman who was starting to see her life as a pattern similar to a fairy story. The archetypal nature of fairy stories was first looked at by Carl Jung and is very popular with students of Joseph Campbell. Although I prefer using the magical imagination and the Inner Kingdom as a good method of looking at archetypes affecting our lives, if we start to see ourselves and others as symbols in the material world, it is inevitable that they will form into patterns that start to look like legends or fairy stories.

It is common in esoteric groups for the leaders to find themselves adopting a mythic status to their role. One common myth they tend to adopt is that of a priest or priestess of Atlantis. Sometimes they, or more often their students, will say they had a previous life in that mythic history. But while Atlantis is seen as a place of magical power, it is also an allegory for magical arrogance, of power misused to gain authority over others. Is it any wonder that, after a while, such people start to become supremely arrogant and insensitive to their peers?

Aleister Crowley cheerfully courted the "Black Magician" image. If the press of the time is to believed, Crowley was the "wickedest man on Earth," who practiced black magic. Anyone reading Crowley's biographies or his autobiography from a psychological profile would be aware that such titles somehow validated him and gave more magical credence to a man than he deserved. Throughout his life, Crowley seemed to want to shock, simply to get attention. Yet living the myth of the "Black Magician" led him to the inevitable Faustian end: alone, drug dependent, and forgotten. If Crowley had adopted another myth, his life might have had a different outcome, but history will always remember him as a evil sorcerer in spite of any cleverness of his magical system or poetry.

I often wonder if John F. Kennedy's life might have been different if he had not taken the Arthurian myth. With his administration labeled "Camelot," and his battles with the military and the FBI (the

"Usurper"), he fits snugly within T. H. White's *The Once and Future King* version of the Arthurian myth, right up to the tragic end of his reign. Theoretically, Kennedy should have been killed by an newly discovered illegitimate son, but being bumped off by someone who wanted control of the country fits into the myth too.

Adolf Hitler, a man for whom myth was of paramount importance, saw himself in the role of Siegfried in Wagner's opera *Der Ring des Nibelungen*, saving the world from the "evil Jewish dwarves." He forgot that the end of that opera has Siegfried and his girlfriend dying in flames as all around them burns and a new order is born without the gods or a master race.

The message of these famous people's lives is to choose your myths carefully, or know when would be a good time to change them. All myths of greatness start with the hero doing well, but generally there is a seed that is overlooked and eventually leads to destruction. Arthur, Roland, Merlin, Theseus, Helen of Troy, Cassandra, and Ophelia all meet bad ends. All had the option of changing their fates, and if you are going to live these myths, then it is important that you learn from them. Be wise like Arthur, but stand up to evil within your kingdom; be brave like Roland, but don't be suicidal; find your treasure like Jason, but don't deceive another to get it. It is important to remember that your gender has nothing to do with the myth you are living. I know several females who are living out the myth of Hercules and of Merlin. Likewise, one of my male friends is living his life as if he were Helen of Troy!

And They Lived Happily Ever After

By seeing the material world as a legend, and by looking directly at our internal myths in pathworkings and meditation, we are in a powerful position to forge our lives into the shape we want. We can stand like the archetypal Mage as a link between Heaven and Earth. With symbols as our magic wands, we no longer have to have our universe shaped by the neurotic programming of our childhood or early teens. We can find within ourselves our own counsel and guides, and free ourselves from the weakness of our teachers, friends, and family. Without fear we can build an Inner Kingdom of peace, and then see it manifest in our environment outside us. Everything we do or see around us becomes a reflection of our inner state and can be seen as the Universal Mind teaching us how to be more than human.

The key to "living happily ever after," or at least individual fulfillment, is that divine gift of imagination. Life is a dream, so make sure yours is a good one.

Endnotes

Chapter One

1. Esoteric Order of the Golden Dawn Flying Roll V.

2. Simon and Schuster, 1994 edition.

3. Bill Hicks, who died in 1994, was a so-called "shock comedian" who, in my view, made accurate observations on political, social, and spiritual situations. The fact that he could do that and get a laugh was incredible.

4. This is what psychologists call classic conditioning. Psychological tests on children are now considered about as ethical as bearbaiting.

5. Carl Gustav Jung was an associate of Freud, the founder of modern psychoanalysis. He broke with Freud after emphasizing the role of symbolism in the unconscious.

6. I use the term loosely. Archetypal figures had been a key part of magical tradition for centuries and Jung simply redefined them. He was then able to go back through the huge amount of occult and alchemical literature and point out the archetypal figures to a round of applause from his students.

7. The Esoteric Order of the Golden Dawn Flying Roll Number V, Imagination, by Dr Berridge.

8. I am, of course, referring to the four cabbalistic worlds.

9. I don't believe a word of it, as it is a common position in Egyptian statues. There is one image I have seen that shows the so-called meditator with his wife, with her arm around him, which is not really indicative of a good meditation session. Still, the sitting on a chair is the most comfortable position without being so comfortable that you fall asleep!

10. English people will, of course, use a "lift" instead of an "elevator."

11. This is an extremely powerful Greek name of God, and it is said that vibrating the name opens a connection with the divine force behind the universe. It is also considered by some sources as a vibration formula to open a gate to the fourth dimension.

12. Although there is an outside chance you might call this soldier Vim, Flash, Jif, Mr. Clean, or some other household cleaner.

13. Routledge & Kegan Paul, London, 1996.

14. Mercury rules computing.

Chapter Two

1. I will not reveal the name of this group because part of this early ritual is still being practiced as part of a particularly powerful initiation system.

2. There is a tendency to believe that the Esoteric Order of the Golden Dawn, or the Golden Dawn, was called the Hermetic Order of the Golden Dawn. However, according to historical paperwork, I have seen the original group was either called the Esoteric or the less catchy Golden Dawn (by members). The name "Hermetic Order of the Golden Dawn" was first coined by Israel Regardie and adopted by some of the modern resurrections of the order he helped to establish in the 1980s. Since then, a number of modern Golden Dawn groups have been established, and although the Esoteric Order collapsed at the beginning of the twentieth

century, it is surprising how many of these new groups attempt to gain kudos by claiming direct descent from the original group. If they really were direct descendants, they would not call themselves "Hermetic Order," but would refer to themselves using the original name. (Since I first mentioned this issue of the name of the Esoteric Order of the Golden Dawn in my book *Making Talismans*, there has been sudden upswing in the numbers of groups advertising themselves as the Esoteric Order!) After the Esoteric Order collapsed, it divided into three different groups: the Alpha et Omega, the Holy Order of the Golden Dawn, and the Stella Matutina. Of the three, only the Stella Matutina continued to teach practical magic, finally shutting its doors in New Zealand in the late 1970s. All these groups used the same rituals. However, although much of the teaching was the same, the emphasis varied from group to group.

3. These were called Flying Rolls.

4. Flying Roll Number IV.

5. So no surprises there!

6. These are air elementals, called sylphs. The sphere of Foundation is attributed to the element of air.

7. The late William Grey was an inspired magician, and was responsible for a number of interesting developments in the British magical scene. However, he proudly held some views that were not politically correct.

8. The kernel of this system was published by a former Servants of the Light supervisor David Goddard in his book *Tower of Alchemy*.

9. This is an English transliteration and the *Th* is the Hebrew letter Tau.

10. *The Ancient Egyptian Pyramid Texts*, R. O. Faulkner, Oxford University Press, 1969, p. 99.

11. There was one esoteric group who had an elderly member who decided to die during a pathworking and no one realized what had happened until they all came back. It was assumed that he was concentrating adequately and did not die in his sleep.

Chapter Three

1. We will be examining the use of legend in magical imagination later in this book.

2. I am uncertain if he was the king or Cromwell in this one, but he never really struck me as the type that would lose his head!

3. Before anyone complains about the stilted nature of the writing of this particular pathworking, I should point out that it is written to be read in a pathworking. Some sentences are designed for emphasis.

4. The partner can be male or female. It should not be someone who is "real."

5. In Celtic society, women fought for the defense of their village or land.

6. Just like there is no point going to an alternative healer to have your aura repaired if you are just going to allow someone to damage it again.

7. What had happened was the woman had concentrated on finding more friends and developing a social life now that the abuser was out of her life. This made her feel much more self-confident, which healed her. In other words, the villagers (her friends) had made her feel better.

8. Remember that money is a symbol of your power, energy, and time. You may find yourself having to give money to a being in the outside world. This will indicate that you must be prepared to spend time, energy, and effort toward that cause in real life.

9. In this case it was probably a representation of the writer's feminine creative side or Muse.

Chapter Four

1. Like most things in the occult world, this was affectionately shortened by the practicing group into the phrase "psycho-magic."

2. "Rosarium Philosophorum" was in *De Alchemia Opuscula complura veterum philosophorum* . . . , Frankfurt, 1550.

3. My mother always said this worked well until I started to question my parents.

4. Colin was used to pathworking and was comfortable about allowing these inner characters to suggest their own cure. This is risky, as the inner character might only suggest the obvious intellectual answer. In this case, it would have been to bury the bishop, which would have been a bad psychological symbol, as it would have suggested repressing the force rather than integration. This would not have shown the acceptance and re-integration of the bishop symbol into a positive affirmation for change.

5. If the person is aware of his or her problem, several of the words in this sequence should specifically reflect that knowledge.

6. The conversation will probably be more involved than this. You should not feel bound to the script so long as you follow its general points.

Chapter Five

1. A copy of the legend was painted on the temple walls at Edfu, in Egypt. It was translated by Margaret Murray in *Ancient Egyptian Legends* (John Murray, London, 1913).

Chapter Six

1. King James Bible, Ezekiel 1: verses 4, 5, 27, and 28.

2. *Interior Castle* Chapter 2.

3. *Elements of Mysticism*, R. A. Gilbert, 1991, Element Books.

4. *Ascent of Mount Carmel*. Trans. E. Allison Peers Book 1, Chapter 13, Paragraph 12.

5. *The Imitation of Christ*. Trans. Richard Whitford, modernized by Harold C. Gardiner. New York: Doubleday, 1955, p. 58.

6. Meister Eckhart's *Sermons and Treatises,* Vol II, translated by M. O. C. Walshe (1979).

7. Although I still think this is an interesting idea, I would not do it in that form now nor do I quite see "contacts" in the way I did then.

Chapter Seven

1. Flying Roll IV (S. L. MacGregor Mathers). Private Golden Dawn papers.

2. *The Sorcerer and His Apprentice* (Aquarian Press, 1983), by R. A. Gilbert.

3. My book *Making Talismans* (Llewellyn, St Paul, 2001) contains more detailed information on flashing tablets.

4. A list of gods and goddesses and their symbols can be found in my book *Making Talismans* (Llewellyn, St. Paul, 2001).

Bibliography

Agrippa, Henry Cornelius. *Three Books of Occult Philosophy.* Edited by Donald Tyson. St. Paul, MN: Llewellyn Publishing, 1995.

Ashcroft-Nowicki, Dolores. *Inner Landscapes.* London, UK: Aquarian, 1989.

———. *Highways of the Mind.* London, UK: Aquarian, 1987.

———. *Shining Paths.* Loughborough, UK: Thoth Publishing, 2002.

Butler, W. E. *The Magician, His Training and Work.* London, UK: Aquarian, 1959.

Cambell, Joseph. *The Hero with a Thousand Faces.* Princeton, NJ: Princeton University Press, 1973.

Farrell, Nick. *Making Talismans.* St. Paul, MN: Llewellyn Publishing, 2001.

Fortune, Dion. *Mystical Qabalah.* London, UK: Williams and Norgate, 1935.

Gilbert, R. A. *Elements of Mysticism.* Shaftsbury, UK: Element, 1991.

Goddard, David. *Tower of Alchemy.* York Beach, ME: Weiser, 1999.

King, Francis. *Ritual Magic of the Golden Dawn.* Rochester, VT: Destiny Books, 1997.

Knight, Gareth. *A Practical Guide to Cabbalistic Symbolism.* York Beach, ME: Weiser, 1969.

———. *Experience of the Inner Worlds.* Toddington, UK: Helios Book Service, 1975.

———. *Dion Fortune and the Inner Light.* Loughborough, UK: Thoth Publications, 2000.

Lilly, W. *Christian Astrology.* 1647. Reprint, Exeter, UK: Regulus.

Mathers, S. L. MacGregor. *The Key of Solomon the King.* 1888. Reprint, translated by S. Liddell MacGregor Mathers, York Beach, ME: Weiser, 1986.

Matthews, Caitlen and John. *The Western Way.* London, UK: Arkana, 1985.

Masters, REL, and Jean Housten. *Mind Games.* Wellingborough, UK: Turnstone Press, 1983.

Melling, David J. *Understanding Plato.* Oxford, UK: Oxford University Press, 1987.

Person, Ethel. *The Force of Fantasy.* London, UK: Harper Collins, 1997.

Raff, Jeffrey. *Jung and the Alchemical Imagination.* York Beach, ME: Nicholas Hayes, 2000.

Regardie, Israel. *The Golden Dawn.* 6th Edition. St. Paul, MN: Llewellyn Publications, 1990.

Yates, Frances A. *The Art of Memory.* London, UK: Pimlico, 1966.

Van der Post, Laurens. *Jung and the Story of our Time.* London, UK: The Scientific Book Club, 1977.

Free Magazine

Read unique articles by Llewellyn authors, recommendations by experts, and information on new releases. To receive a **free** copy of Llewellyn's consumer magazine, *New Worlds of Mind & Spirit,* simply call 1-877-NEW-WRLD or visit our website at www.llewellyn.com and click on *New Worlds.*

LLEWELLYN ORDERING INFORMATION

Order Online:
Visit our website at www.llewellyn.com, select your books, and order them on our secure server.

Order by Phone:
- Call toll-free within the U.S. at 1-877-NEW-WRLD (1-877-639-9753). Call toll-free within Canada at 1-866-NEW-WRLD (1-866-639-9753).
- We accept VISA, MasterCard, and American Express

Order by Mail:
Send the full price of your order (MN residents add 7% sales tax) in U.S. funds, plus postage & handling to:

Llewellyn Worldwide
P.O. Box 64383, Dept. 0-7387-0407-5
St. Paul, MN 55164-0383, U.S.A.

Postage & Handling:

Standard (U.S., Mexico, & Canada). If your order is:
Up to $25.00, add $3.50
$25.01 - $48.99, add $4.00
$49.00 and over, FREE STANDARD SHIPPING
(Continental U.S. orders ship UPS. AK, HI, PR, & P.O. Boxes ship USPS 1st class. Mex. & Can. ship PMB.)

International Orders:
Surface Mail: For orders of $20.00 or less, add $5 plus $1 per item ordered. For orders of $20.01 and over, add $6 plus $1 per item ordered.

Air Mail:
Books: Postage & Handling is equal to the total retail price of all books in the order.
Non-book items: Add $5 for each item.

Orders are processed within 2 business days.
Please allow for normal shipping time. Postage and handling rates subject to change.

MAKING TALISMANS
Living Entities of Power

NICK FARRELL

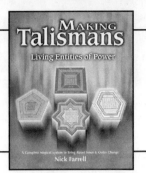

A complete magical system to bring about inner and outer change.

Making Talismans gives you the secret keys and practical techniques to turn mundane objects into "living entities of power," bringing real change in your life. By pooling magical practices from areas as diverse as shamanism, paganism, the Esoteric Order of the Golden Dawn, and Dion Fortune, *Making Talismans* trains you in techniques from the simplest to the most complex until you can perform advanced magical talismanic operations.

You will learn what talismans are and how they work; a brief history of talismans in the Western Mystery Tradition; how to use names of power, angels, magical languages, and color magic; how to draw talismans, consecrate them, and even banish them.

0–7387–0004–5, 240 pp., 7½ x 9⅛, illus.　　　　　　　**$14.95**

To order, call 1-877-NEW-WRLD
Prices subject to change without notice